SHALLOW GRAVES

For 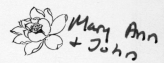 *Mary Ann + John*

TWO WOMEN
AND VIETNAM

with love from

Wendy Wilder Larsen

Tran Thi Nga

Wendy Wilder Larsen
1989

PERENNIAL LIBRARY

Harper & Row, Publishers, New York
Cambridge, Philadelphia, San Francisco, Washington
London, Mexico City, São Paulo, Singapore, Sydney

A hardcover edition of this book is published by Random House, Inc. It is here reprinted by arrangement with Random House, Inc.

Portions of this work first appeared in *Hawaii Review* and *13th Moon*.

Grateful acknowledgment is made to the following for permission to reprint previously published material:

The Asia Society: "Poor Matchmaking" and excerpts from "Lament of the Warrior's Wife," published in *A Thousand Years of Vietnamese Poetry,* ed. by Nguyen Ngoc Bich, tr. by Burton Raffel and W. S. Merwin. Alfred A. Knopf, Inc. 1975.

Columbia Pictures Publications: Excerpts from the lyrics to "Fire and Rain" by James Taylor, Copyright © 1969, 1970 by Blackchord Music, Inc., and Country Road Music, Inc. Administered by Blackchord Music, Inc.

Farrar, Straus & Giroux, Inc., and Faber & Faber, Ltd.: Excerpt from "Losses," by Randall Jarrell. From *The Complete Poems of Randall Jarrell.* Copyright 1948, renewed copyright © 1975 by Mrs. Randall Jarrell. Reprinted by permission of the publishers.

The New York Public Library: One-page excerpt from "The Vietnamese Language," by Nguyen Dinh Hoa, Vietnam Culture Series, No. 2, 1961. Reprinted by permission of the General Research Division, The New York Public Library, Astor, Lenox and Tilden Foundations.

Warner Bros. Music: Lyrics excerpted from "Ballad of a Thin Man," by Bob Dylan. © 1965 Warner Bros, Inc. All rights reserved. Used by permission.

Library of Congress Cataloging-in-Publication Data

Larsen, Wendy Wilder, 1940–
   Shallow graves.

   "Perennial Library."
   1. Vietnamese Conflict, 1961–1975—Poetry. I. Tran, Thi Nga, 1927–   . II. Title.
[PS3562.A745S5   1987]   811'.54   86-46077
ISBN 0-06-097093-6 (pbk.)

87 88 89 90 91 MPC 10 9 8 7 6 5 4 3 2 1

TO
Nguyen Ṭhi Toan
Nguyen Hung Vuong
Katherine Burton
Katharine Herrick Metcalf

Kunming

CHINA

N

Red River

Yen Bai

Dien
Bien Phu

Vinh Yen

HANOI

Hadong

Haiphong

Gulf
of
Tonkin

NORTH VIETNAM

PLAIN
OF JARS

LAOS

Vientiane

17TH PARALLEL

THAILAND

Khe Sanh

Quang Tri

Hue

Hamburger Hill

Danang

Ashau
Valley

Firebase
Mary Ann

SOUTH VIETNAM

CAMBODIA

Ban Me
Thuot

Phnom
Penh

Dalat

Bien Hoa

SAIGON

Cholon

Can Tho

CHUONG
THIEN

Miles

0   150

0   Kms.   150

© A·Karl/J·Kemp 1986

FOREWORD

In Vietnam as early as the fifteenth century, it was a common practice for a band of singers, or a single performer—often a blind person—to travel from village to village reciting from a repertoire of verse novels. The verse novel, or *truyen,* is a Vietnamese form, but the stories were adapted from Chinese prose tales. In the spirit of that tradition, I feel like the performer of Tran Thi Nga's story as well as my own.

I first met this remarkable woman in 1970 when I was teaching Shakespeare and Romantic Poetry to Vietnamese teachers at the University of Saigon. I had gone to Vietnam to join my husband, a journalist covering the war. Mrs. Nga was the bookkeeper in his office. She soon became my guide through the maze of life in her country.

In 1971 I left Saigon and began to write poems describing my experience in Vietnam, never expecting to see Mrs. Nga again. But in 1975, days before Saigon fell, she escaped from her country and came to live in America. She called me to say now it was she who needed help.

One day we were having lunch in New York City to celebrate her birthday. I remarked that although we had been friends in Vietnam I had never felt it appropriate to ask her anything about her personal life. It was then she began to tell me about her childhood in North Vietnam, her life in China, her career in South Vietnam—an epic story of courage and survival. By the end of that lunch, we had agreed to work on a book together.

Once a week, sometimes twice, we met and she told me her story, which I recorded on tape. Exiled from her country, she was able to recall poignant images from her lost land and culture. I transformed her memories into narrative verse trying to stay as close to her voice as possible. These poems, added to those I had written about my year in Vietnam, became *Shallow Graves: Two Women and Vietnam.*

—W.W.L.

CONTENTS

BA LARSEN'S
STORY

SAIGON
1970-1971

ASSIGNMENT

I remember the night you came back from dinner
(we were living in Hollywood then)
and said, "It's going to be Vietnam."
Somehow I had pictured London.

As a sophomore, I had gone to hear the Dragon Lady,
Madame Nhu, speak at Harvard.
All I can remember now
is that her dress was brilliant yellow silk
and her red nails so long
they curved backward.

POP! a black-and-white photograph
in my brain
Diem and Nhu, brothers
dead in the back of a truck somewhere
blood streaming from their mouths.

My other images came from television.
I pictured me in a flak jacket
diving down a manhole
dodging shrapnel;
buildings falling
and burning all around me.

I pictured tank patrols in the jungle
booby traps and poison pungi sticks.
Medics lifting wounded soldiers
into waiting helicopters
the wind from the blades
flattening tall grasses
into circles.

Or was that in a movie?

CAPTURE

Vacationing in New England
two weeks before we left,
we got the news:
our predecessor had been captured
a prisoner of the Khmer Rouge
held somewhere in Cambodia.

        I dream I'm running.
        I'm running in a jungle at night.
        Palm trees clatter overhead.
        My feet are bleeding.
        I cannot understand the order.

We took our guests on a picnic
to a meadow near our house.
Their voices crisscrossed
overhead like bees.

"British soldiers,"
my friend said, pointing to lichen
with bright red hats
and straight gray bodies,
"Perfect for your terrarium."

We sat on granite
drinking too much white wine
under an apple tree.

Two mornings before,
I'd watched a fat blue jay
rip the blossoms from that tree
shredding them with such gusto
the pink spilled from his beak.

Alone then,
I heard his satisfied scoldings
patrol the tall grasses of the meadow,
the borders of the woods.

ADVICE

I waited in the hall
on the 24th floor
for my turn to see
the Chief of Correspondents,
my arms shot full
of plague, cholera, yellow fever.
His face floated up
from behind his desk
like one of those answers
in a fortune globe.

"Any questions?" he asked.
"What about the water?"
"People do live there," he said.

A map of the world
big as the wall
the countries tinted blue
the oceans green
spun over his left shoulder.

I focused on pushpins
stuck on the map.
Across the Atlantic
beyond Europe, Turkey, Afghanistan's Hindu Kush
beyond India
down past Thailand
east to the bulge
in a peninsula floating in green
stood two red ones.

One of them would be us.

ADVICE 2

"Call your friend, the expert," my husband said.
"She'll know. She's been out there
and back four times."

I reported her words:
"There are no gynecologists in Vietnam."

"B.Y.O.G.Y.N." My husband laughed.

ADVICE 3

"You'll like it there.
Saigon's not scary at all.
All that humidity's marvelous for the skin
and those wonderful little seamstresses
come to your house, work all day
and eat like gerbils."

SAIGON HOUSEKEEPING

I arrived at Christmas time.
The cook left the first day.
She was part Chinese
would not work with Chi Phuc,
Vietnamese.

I sat in a chair
watching her carry past me
our pots and pans
stainless-steel knives and forks
pottery plates
our colander.

She took the same turns,
one load at a time,
out of the kitchen
across the living room
down the stairs—
an ant to her mound.

I drew the line
at a large earthenware crock
used to hold the water
we boiled each day.
She had somehow strapped it to her back.

When she wasn't looking
I'd get up, throw Hong Kong tinsel
on the Christmas tree
to hang there
with the colored lights
the twisted dragons.

OPERATION FIRST STEPS

"O.K. this is it.
Only a block to the office.
No more standing at the window, kid."

I watched my legs
in a slow replay
move down the dark steps

past the women
washing laundry in plastic tubs,
their voices shrill as shrapnel
caught in the stairwell.

I moved
first right leg, then left
past the one-eyed guard

out onto the street
and the Pacific sun
that hurts on impact,

over the broken concrete,
head down, muttering

                "Step on a crack!
                Break your mother's back"

as if that childhood chant
could make me brave

past vendors
selling packs of stolen Marlboros

our WWII veterans sent from home
complete with messages

> "We in Sioux City, Iowa
> love you boys"

past lepers.
One had a hole in his cheek.

I rounded the corner
touched the white column
of the Continental Palace Hotel
like the home tree in "capture the flag."

From the open veranda
voices breathed behind the potted palms,
behind the gin-and-tonics
that sweated like the soldiers.

I heard my husband,
whom I could talk to,
debriefing the office Vietnamese reporter
on Kill Ratios, Task Forces, ARVN movements in I Corps.

THE GAME

Our first social event
we played a war game
in a journalist's flat
above the market street.

A free-lancer made the rules.
There were cards for troop deployment.
Points for Pacification.
Cards to call in air strikes.

I think my chair
was Quang Tri or Ban Me Thuot.
I can't remember now.

But I took my cards.
I rolled the dice.
I played the game.

LEARNING THE WAR

I never made friends faster.
We foreigners were learning the war,
cramming it in
breakfast, lunch and dinner.

We learned the abbreviations:
USAID, JUSPAO, MACV, DMZ,
ARVN, NLF, GVN.

We learned the names of battles:
Dien Bien Phu
Ashau Valley
Khe Sanh
Hamburger Hill
Firebase Mary Ann.

We peppered our speech
with militarese

with roger this
and roger that
with dust off
blown away and neutralize

to give us courage—
warriors painting our faces
before battle.

We learned to rate hamlets
praise Ruff-Puffs
recognize Kit Carson scouts
laugh at White Mice.

We learned it all
and we couldn't speak to anyone
when we got home.

THE LANGUAGE

    Vietnamese is a tonal language, that is to say, a given syllable may be pronounced in any of the six tones, thus multiplying the number of vocables by six. To take a classic example, **ma**, pronounced in the high level tone, means «ghost». The same word pronounced with the high rising tone refers to the « cheek ». It means « but », « grave », «horse» or «rice seedling», depending on whether it is given the low falling, low rising, broken rising, or low constricted tone, respectively. Following are the six forms of the syllable /**ma**/ pronounced in the six tones :

    ma   má   mà   må   mã   mạ

«ghost» «cheek» «but» «grave» «horse» «rice seedling»

WATCH

Most of the journalists
wore army-issue watches
with large waterproof faces
and khaki-colored straps.

When I got mine on the black market,
I turned it over and read
"This watch is non-maintainable."

SAVING FACE

I had a problem with my staff in Saigon.
The maid, Chi Phuc, my favorite, cried most of the day.
The new cook, higher up the pecking order,
was forcing her to do his chopping, his dishes.
I called the office and spoke to Mrs. Nga,
the only woman there.

"It's 'Nga' like 'ma,'" she corrected me.
I had pronounced it 'naga' like Naugahyde.

"Give me a week," she said
and came up with this solution.

"Scold Chi Phuc in front of the cook.
Say the Big Boss, your husband, is upset.
His laundry isn't getting done perfectly."
I got mad at the person I wasn't mad at,
saved everyone's face
and brought peace to my Asian household.

RIDING TO SCHOOL

I taught literature in Saigon then
at the School of Pedagogy.

My students rode to school on Hondas.

The women wore silk ao dai
black satin pants.

The pastel panels floated out
behind them as they drove

pink, blue, green
like so many dragonfly wings.

They wore black gloves
pale conical hats

tied with maroon ribbons
under their chins.

Their backs were straight.

From my window I wanted to call
like a riding instructor,

"Nice hands. Good seat."

I watched them each morning
drive through the puddles

and park in a circle
under the flamboyant tree.

STAR-CROSSED

They stood when I entered the classroom,
called me Ba Larsen,

which means "Mrs." or "Lady"
a sign of respect.

I concentrated on appearance
and reality, textual analysis of *Romeo and Juliet*.

Late one afternoon Miss Hoa
came to the apartment on Le Thanh Ton.

I remember her white dress
black hair to her waist.

She had never been in an elevator before.

She said she was in love with her cousin
had been since she was thirteen

explained that many Vietnamese love their cousins,
the extended family.

Such love was forbidden by the church.
Should she kill herself like Juliet?

She drank the Coke I offered.

From the balcony we watched
magnesium flares fall beyond the harbor.

TEACHING

My students brought ca dao to class,
folk poems, centuries old,
told over and over
passed on from one generation to another.

      Ca Dao to Hoa Sen   To the Lotus
In the pond there is nothing more beautiful than the lotus.
Green leaves, white petals, yellow anthers.
Yellow anthers, white petals, green leaves.
Growing out of mud, yet not giving off the mud smell.

Trong đầm gì đẹp bằng sen
Lá xanh bông trắng lại chen nhị vàng.
Nhị vàng bông trắng lá xanh
Gần bùn mà chẳng hôi tanh mùi bùn.

I announced:
"Clearly this poem speaks of appearance and reality."

Mr. Thung raised his hand in protest,
"Excuse me, Ba Larsen.
It is you who do not understand.
We live here.
We know the lotus flower
grows in stinky mud.
For us, the poem's about reality.
For you, who do not know our land,
it is about appearances."

STUDENT PAPER

I have to say that ca dao cannot be translated. It's the meaning and the feeling it gives to the reader that forbids the translation. Only people in the Vietnamese culture can fully understand and enjoy ca dao, but I will give you my favorite.

> *"Oh my darling, over there by the side of the path,*
> *why do you scoop up and throw away yellow moonlight*
> *shining on the water's surface?"*

This is a question on a summer moonlit night asked by a passer-by to a hard-working young girl using her draining can to take water from a flooded field to a dry field.

TO MARKET, TO MARKET

Scared to enter the big market, that noisy covered maze, alone,
I asked Mrs. Nga if she would be my guide.

She showed me the fruit ladies, seated on their platforms
among pyramids of mangosteens, papayas and smelly durian.

Heads wrapped in turbans, teeth red with betel,
they balanced their brass scales

bartering in high-pitched voices like so many exotic birds,
like puppets banging their heads together.

She led me through hot tunnels. No air.
Things jostled from all sides. Chairs hung from the ceiling.

Everywhere the smell of scallions and ginger
the stench of meat rotting in the sun.

We threaded our way. Black catfish flopped on the tile floor.
Crabs wriggled their blue claws through slats in straw baskets.

Tiny striped snails clung to the sides of aluminum buckets.
Her favorite fish vendor smiled the red-toothed smile of easy money.

We pressed past bins of turmeric and cloves, bolts of lavender and
    tangerine silk,
opium trays, black-market Kiwi shoe polish, Chinese blue-and-white
    porcelain

past one woman who sold individual garlic buds
displayed on a plaid handkerchief.

Exhausted, we collapsed into a pedi-cab and let an old man
pedal us home through noonday heat.

Over the market, a huge suspended sign floated:
a smiling black man with enormous white teeth

advertising Hynos, a Vietnamese toothpaste. She told me
"All Vietnamese know that blacks have the whitest teeth."

MULTIPLES

Along the Bien Hoa Highway
I saw shacks
made from aluminum sheets.

In the USA, we cut the metal
into soda-pop cans
that we toss on the side of our roads.

Here, for miles and miles
their red and green houses
spelled out *Coca-Cola   7 Up*.

CALLING HOME

I called my family from the USO
decorated like a high school gym.
Chains of red white and blue crepe paper
sagged in the heat.
The room was thick with the smell of fries
Osterizers blending chocolate shakes
the snap of shuffled cards.

I'd wait in line
with GI's sweating half-circles
down to their khaki waists.
Together we'd count the time difference
to the States.

"We're all sitting in the blue room
on my big bed upstairs,"
I heard my mother's voice
break over the line
like surf over rocks.
"The ducks and geese are flying.
You know how I dread September."

September—Rhode Island.
I pictured my family on cool evenings
rocking on the porch
in black wicker chairs
under Japanese lanterns.
The lawn curved down to the rocks
where the fishermen waited in the fog
for the blues to come in.

That morning in my dream
our white frame house stood
at the edge of a jungle.
Its windows lit up
like a child's eyes.

CONSCIOUSNESS-RAISING

Saigon was a natural place
to start a consciousness-raising group.
We were eight women
all wives of journalists.

I remember sitting in a hot small room
a punkah fan creaking overhead,
our knees forming a circle
as we discussed why baby girls
are dressed in pink,
boys in blue.

Outside, a peasant woman
driven into the city by the bombing
slept in the street
on a newspaper
a child pulling at her breast.

BOYS

This is the land
where they dye eggs red
when a son is born.

This is the land
where the birth of a boy
brings a week's celebration.

In this land
when a girl is born
the mother is quiet.

ASSIGNMENT FROM BA LARSEN

Compare William Blake's "London" to Saigon in 1970

LONDON

I wander thro' each charter'd street,
Near where the charter'd Thames does flow,
And mark in every face I meet
Marks of weakness, marks of woe.

In every cry of every Man,
In every Infant's cry of fear,
In every voice, in every ban,
The mind-forg'd manacles I hear.

Now the Chimney-sweeper's cry
Every black'ning Church appalls,
And the hapless Soldier's sigh
Runs in blood down Palace walls.

But most thro' midnight streets I hear
How the youthful Harlot's curse
Blasts the new born Infant's tear,
And blights with plagues the Marriage hearse.

—William Blake

STUDENT'S RESPONSE

Where is the traditional and peaceful Saigon?
Where is the Pearl of the Orient—that sweet name?

In every street I see bar-girls in mini-skirts
shocking every passer-by.

At midnight I hear feverish jazz music
rocking with the pounding of the far-away cannons.

I smell in every corner the stink of scattered garbage.

Corruption touches every level of society
while the poor starve.

Where is the Pearl of the Orient?

Refugees bombed from their villages fill her sidewalks.
Pollution and horns disturb her treeless avenues.

Large foreigners live in her houses.
Men in green uniforms patrol her streets, sleep with her women.

Juveniles, uprooted from their families, steal from her people.
The rush of disorder shows on every face.

I wish I had not been born to live in this time.

I am worn out.
My city is worn out.
My country is worn out.

PROTOCOL

Downstairs, at the embassy party,
there were place cards with embossed gold crests
antimacassars on the backs of stuffed chairs
talk of commitment.

Upstairs, in the bedroom after dinner,
there was a refrigerator filled with champagne
and bar-girls dancing
to Mick Jagger's rock 'n' roll.

"Welcome to the turd world,"
the diplomat winked.

BAR-GIRL'S SONG TO A GI

I love you beaucoup.
You love me titi.
You give me baby.
I give you V.D.

MONEY TALKS

The office had a fixer.
Nothing he couldn't do.

His bag of tricks was exquisite.
If your smallpox vaccination expired,
he got you the stamp
without the office visit.

When our colleague was caught
with marijuana for example
he said, "You're doing a story on drugs
say you were collecting samples."

He could save you from jail
from any disaster,
get you through customs
in under two hours.

All you needed
was an extra briefcase of piasters.

FOR CHI PHUC

You ironed my shirts
in my living room.
Two women
in one apartment.
You ironed.
I read about your country.
We could not speak one word to each other.
When you almost died
of your eighth pregnancy at 27,
I found you at home sitting on a rush mat.
Your deserter husband
hid behind a wardrobe
plastered with *Playboy* centerfolds.
I took you to the Tan Son Nhut Hospital.
When they laid you on the gurney cart
and I saw you in my missing silk underpants
you shrugged.

A NAME

In Vietnamese,
Mrs. Nga explained,
chi means "maid" or "sister"
depending on the relationship.

I thought it was a name.

CHI AI

Ai, the seamstress, was creepy.
She weighed as much as a mynah bird
and looked like one.
She could copy anything.
She stopped sewing
only to eat plain rice,
nothing on it.
She'd swish the last kernel
from her bowl
with cold brown tea.

My mother's words
floated up to me
like lyrics from some song.

> "Eat everything on your plate.
> Remember the starving children of China."

I was told this over bowls of oatmeal
brown sugar and heavy cream.
At the bottom of the dish,
Beatrix Potter's Peter Rabbit,
the prize for finishing.

JEANNETTE

Jeannette stopped by "the Nam"
on her way home
from temples in Burma.
Each morning the seamstress
came to her villa
fitting the tea-colored pajamas
until they lay on her body—a silk skin.

"Darling, why bother teaching them English?
We taught them French.
Next they will have to learn Russian."
She knew her antiques.
"Not that one," she'd roar,
pointing to a blue-and-white teapot,
"that's early Chiang Kai-shek."

She wore a Nikkormat
around her neck
like an ornament.
Her portraits of us
came out silhouettes.
She took her readings on the sun.

ORPHANAGE

When I visited the orphanage
I went with balloons, hard candies
old *National Geographics*.

The children grabbed for everything.
I gave one a candy, others screamed
until seven or eight were clawing at my legs.

They popped the balloons
choked on the candies
shredded the magazines.

I looked over to the nun for help.

She stopped ladling gruel into the communal trough
put down the long tin spoon
and came across the room to tell me,

"Next time, if you come,
bring enough for everyone, or bring nothing."

THE WHEEL OF BRIE

For my first office party
I hunted down a wheel of Brie.
When none of the Vietnamese touched it,
I called Mrs. Nga, who told me:

"Some Vietnamese hate dairy products.
We like fruit and vegetables.
We think you Americans
smell of rich butter and milk."

POTTERY FACTORIES

One Thursday each month
my friends and I hired a CBS car
to visit pottery factories in "friendly" villages.

A family enterprise—children carried parts
of clay elephants on boards
placed on their heads

the trunk, the ears, the legs
all separate—carried in procession
an offering to be assembled and fired in the kilns.

In the last stages, tiny boys kneeled
beside the glazed green elephants
painting their toenails gold.

A river flowed by the factory.
We watched narrow boats being loaded
with hundreds of plates and saucers for the city.

Across the river on a porch above the bank
a grandmother rocked a baby in a hammock
by a string attached to her big toe.

"Their babies never cry," my friend said.

On the way back, I coveted her bowls,
the ones with the dancing roosters painted on the sides.
She admitted later she wanted mine with the dragons.

PIDGIN

Bob worked with Brown and Root,
carved out the roads we left there
with earthmovers flown from home.

He had an affair
with a bar-girl called Twiggy
he said spoke only pidgin.

They giggled a lot.
Took Polaroids of each other.
Studied them and giggled some more.

When they came to my apartment,
she said, "You remind me of a housewife.
I remind myself of that flower"—

and pointed to a single red rose
in a tall green vase.

DAVE'S OCELOT

Dave, our journalist friend,
bought a baby ocelot
from the animal market.

Before he got home,
the rain had washed away
its spots.

WINNING THEIR HEARTS
AND MINDS

We rehearsed our *Macbeth*
four scenes from four acts.
I'd cast Lady Macbeth, Banquo, the witches.

They made costumes
bought knives as daggers
memorized their lines.

The day of the performance
the first act was perfect.
I sat proudly in the back.

For Act II
a second Lady Macbeth appeared,
another Banquo, different witches.

Stunned, I spoke to them
when it was all over.
They said their way was more democratic.

I told my friend the expert.

"Calm down," she said.
"You'll get it. But here's a hint.
There are 50 daily newspapers in Saigon."

SHRINE

I played tennis at the Cercle Sportif
with one of the justices of the Supreme Court—
the only Vietnamese to ask me
to his house for dinner.

In the living room
his refrigerator
covered in a blue brocade cloth
was locked.

THE HONDA REVOLUTION

Looking down from my window
I watched lovers
seated on their motorbikes
kissing under the sacred banyan tree.

At siesta, the woman who guarded the bikes
took her nap, lying across the seats
a cone-shaped hat over face.

I played a game with my friend—
who could count
the most people on one Honda.

At Tet, I counted seven
including a grandmother and presents.
I won.

THE HOUSE ON TU DO STREET

*"Something is happening here,
but you don't know what it is.
Do you, Mr. Jones?"*
—*Ballad of a Thin Man*
BOB DYLAN

We called their place
on Tu Do Street "the crash pad."
It had been Graham Greene's.

Something was always going on there
not the John-Wayne-rerun
frozen-chicken-à-la-king-French-poodle
white-wall-to-wall carpeting
of the American compound.

They were young Americans
who came to Vietnam and stayed.
Sam came in the army
worked for an alternative news service.
Skye read me my first ca dao.
She knew the language
had her baby in a Vietnamese hospital.

More Vietnamese than the Vietnamese
they hunkered down
on the backs of their calves to chat
slept on the floor
ate with wooden chopsticks
made cha gio and pho.

There was a difference.
Rolling papers lay among their dictionaries.
Our go-betweens
they knew the way to opium
as well as Buddha's path.

DAO DUA THE COCONUT MONK

The Dao Dua picked Sam
to be his American successor.
One weekend he led us on his dark-red motorcycle
out into the countryside.

From the brown river, Paradise Island,
the Dao Dua's kingdom, rose like a mirage—
a river platform with painted dragons,
spiral staircases and strings of colored lights.

Monks in maroon and brown pajamas,
their hair pulled forward like elves' caps,
made bells from bullet casings,
grew their trees in jerry cans.

The Dao Dua prayed for peace for ten years.
He lived in two symbolic towers;
slept in Hanoi, prayed in Saigon.
Beneath him lay a papier-mâché map of Vietnam.

Hearing the astronauts had gone to the moon,
he had himself lifted in a basket.
All day people came to him for advice
though he had not spoken in five years.

I climbed the tower to bring him *Life* magazine.
He found a colored picture of Disneyland at night,
pointed out over his world and smiled.

We wore maroon pajamas all day
slept on the floor
with a plastic brick for a pillow.
Monks left bowls of vegetables outside the door.

In the candlelight Sam made a shadow figure
of a praying mantis on the wall.
The insect danced higher and higher
until I heard him say,

"Our countries are both whores.
We deserve each other."
The sound of bells drifted over the river
answered by gunshots from the shore.

WORDY

I had been teaching "wordiness." My students' essays dripped with "It can be said of the mannerisms of Romeo that he had a violent personality."

At the end of the hour, I asked Mr. Phuc to comment on Romeo's speech:

> *Two of the fairest stars in all the heaven,*
> *Having some business, do entreat her eyes*
> *To twinkle in their spheres till they return.*
> *What if her eyes were there, they in her head?*
> *The brightness of her cheek would shame those stars,*
> *As daylight doth a lamp.*

"Shakespeare is wordy," he said, making the whole class laugh.

MILITARY INTERPRETER'S HANDBOOK

The Vietnamese words
for "birthday suit"
were translated
"Nude as a worm in a cocoon."

"Send to Siberia" as
"Send to the place
where the monkeys cough
and the flamingos sing."

Two-bit   *Rẻ tiền*
Two bits   *25 xu*
Two-time   *Đánh lừa*
Typewriter   *Tiểu liên*

U

U-drive-it car   *Xe hơi cho thuê khóng tài-xế*
Unbleached American   *Người Mỹ da đen*
Uncle benny   *Tiệm cầm đồ*
Uncle sam's pokey   *Nhà ngục liên-bang*
Undercover   *Bí-mật*
Unky   *Chú, bác*
Unscramble   *Mã-dịch một điện-văn*
Up-and-upper   *Người liêm-khiết*
Upchuck   *Nôn-oẹ*

V

Varnish remover   *Cà-phê pha thật đậm*
V.D. (Venereal Disease)   *Bệnh lậu*
Vetmobile   *Xe hơi đặc-biệt dành cho **các** thương-binh què quặt*
Vice cops   *Cảnh-sát kiểm-tục*
V.I.P. (Very Important People)   *Những nhân-vật rất quan-trọng*
V.U.P. (Very Unimportant People)   *Những người rất tầm thường*

W

Wade in   *Bắt đầu*
Wage hike   *Tăng lương*

Walking dandruff	*Chấy, rận*
Wampum	*Tiền*
War-hawks	*Người theo phe diều-hâu, chủ chiến*
War horse	*Chính-trị-gia lão thành*
Waterloo	*Thất-bại, sự thất trận*
When my ship comes in	*Khi nào tôi giàu*
When the cows give beer	*Không bao giờ*
Whodidit	*Tiều-thuyết hay là phim trinh-thám*
Whodunist	*Tác-giả tiều-thuyết hay là phim trinh-thám*
Why, sure !	*Là cái chắc !*
Wobbly hole	*Số không (xe hơi)*
Wooden overcoat	*Áo quần*

X

X-eyes	*Mắt lé*

Y

Yes-man	*Người ba phải*
Y-gun	*Đại-bác chống tàu ngầm*
You are all wet	*Anh nhầm to rồi*
You are so right !	*Anh nói đúng quá !*
You bet !	*Dĩ nhiên rồi !*

Z

Zipper your kisser	*Im họng đi !*
Zipper	*Nhanh nhẹn*

DINNER PARTY

I asked my brother, who came out to stay,
what he would like for dinner.
The cook, I told him, could produce
French, Chinese or American.

"Why not Japanese?" he joked.
"Too short an occupation?
No time to teach the culinary arts?"

"Duck *à l'orange*," I ordered
in French that made the cook wince.

That afternoon, my brother watched three ducks,
one white, two black-and-white,
follow the cook up the balcony steps
into the kitchen.

He left the house to avoid
what he knew was coming.

The next morning, inside the refrigerator,
he found a glass of fresh dark blood
drained from their necks.

LETTER FROM MY BROTHER

Dear Wendy,

Back in my own time-zone, the journey has come full circle, and all that is left is great memories, a little better understanding, 18 cases of photographs and incoming American Express bills.

I feel like a returning veteran filled with stories of war and horror. But perhaps the real horror of the thing was to be in a city where war is taken so for granted. I guess really it's no different here, where we watch killing every night before dinner and let it bounce off into inaction.

I find myself viewing more closely not so much for answers, but places that are familiar. I guess I've forsaken all answers, but at least I know now where Vietnam ends and Cambodia begins and that there are real people living there and that they don't all look alike.

Our latest "confrontation" is that our neighbors who think *Hair* is "disgusting" think that we are disgusting too for letting our kids go to see it. It takes all kinds.

I'm watching the news now and you wouldn't believe the height of Tricia Nixon's wedding cake.

You were a great guide. Keep the blood out of the icebox.

Your cowardly brother,

Michael

CHECK-POINTS

Hot nights we'd lie awake
in a room that smelled of mildew and insecticide
watching the blade of the punkah turn overhead,
listening to the rumble of outgoing in the distance,
waiting for Linh, the telex operator, to call from the office.

In the reign of a previous bureau chief
Linh had called in the night
to check on the name of a town.

Awakened, the former Big Boss hollered into the phone:

"You can tell those bastards in New York
in case they've forgotten, there's 13 hours difference between
there and Saigon. That makes it 4 A.M. here.
If they expect me to get up and get dressed
in the middle of the night and walk alone after curfew
through these rat-infested streets to check-point some fact
in a story they'll never run. You can tell them."

In the morning when he came into the office
he saw Linh had telexed his message verbatim.

THE LION

Before breakfast when it was still cool
I joined my neighbor on her roof
for Yoga exercises.

In turquoise leotards and black tights
we crouched,
hands dug into our knees like claws,

then crossed our wide-open eyes
stuck our tongues out and down
as far as we could, leaned forward

and roared into the Saigon air—
two blue Danskin lions
panting to lift our sagging chins.

HOARDING

My friend the expert downstairs
lived in Asia 13 years.
She knew the ropes.

When the PX got in artichokes
she'd call. We'd hire a car
and race to secure one case each.

Sometimes she didn't call till she got back.

VIETNAMESE CA DAO

Buffalo, listen to me.
Go to the fields and work with me.
Plowing is the farmer's destiny.
Here I am. There you are.
Neither of us complains of hard work.
If the rice still has flower,
you still have grass in the field to eat.

PHNOM PENH
AND
VIENTIANE

THE ROYAL HOTEL

The sign at the Phnom Penh airport warned,
"It is unsafe to visit Angkor Wat."

We were driven in a white Mercedes
to the Royal Hotel
where waiters in white uniforms
carried tall drinks
to us journalists sprawled in lounge chairs
by the swimming pool.

In huge rooms upstairs
we spread out maps of Cambodia on the floor
dotted with names of towns and rivers
we couldn't pronounce
without interpreters.

INCOMING

The night they shelled the airport I was there.
I hadn't meant to be. I was on my way to the hotel.

No time, the journalist driving said. He'd been cleaning
grass with his headphones on, almost missed the shelling.

The guards that stopped us were fourteen-year-olds.
They held their weapons like heavy toys.

I was dressed in a light-blue Lilly Pulitzer dress
and open-toed sandals.

From the pitch-black night, someone yelled
"Get down. That's incoming."

I remember thinking the Asians are all in front of the wall,
everyone else crouched behind it. Which was better?

I guess I asked too many times.
A man yelled, "Get down and shut up."

Something heavy whistled overhead.
It came too fast to be scared.

I thought, who's out there in the dark?
who are those guys?
who wants to kill me?

and then came rage
and the shakes
and Oh God please get me out of this.

In the distance the fuel tanks exploded
shooting huge orange balls into the air.

One of the network men got up and screamed
to his Korean camera crew, "Get closer. I want you closer."

and then, "I don't know what possesses me at times like this.
Maybe it's the Devil."

With that he jumped the wall and ran toward the fire
his right arm circling a cavalry charge.

DAWN SOW

After hours, I heard a grunt.
Lifting my face from the dirt,
I watched a pink sow in the half light
slog toward me through a mud puddle,
her enormous swollen tits
touching the ground,
her six piglets squealing behind her.

I remember laughing,
I'm alive.
There's a pig coming toward me.
I'm alive.
There's a pig and her babies coming toward me.

As the sun came up,
I saw the silhouettes of families,
hundreds of them on the one road
leaving their homes,
the men pulling crude wagons
filled with their children,
chickens, a prized sewing machine.

There was an awful stillness
except for the typing of the Reuters man
kneeling by the side of the road
his blue portable on a turned-over crate.

PHNOM PENH DANCING CLASS

The day after the rocket attack
I went alone to the palace

to watch a dancing class
forty children, aged three to fourteen

their purple harem pants
tucked into orange cummerbunds.

Bare curve of shoulder
backs as straight as bamboo

they practiced hour after hour
forcing their delicate fingers back.

An old woman clipped them lovingly
on the ankles with her stick.

All morning, birds flew in and out
resting on the wooden carvings

of the coffered ceiling.
A breeze blew across the river

over the palms
onto the open gallery.

The only sounds were the gamelan—
clear notes trickling over each other

like stream water over rocks—
and the tap tap tapping of the teacher's stick.

THE ROYAL THRONE ROOM

It was not dying—no, not ever dying;
But the night I died I dreamed that I was dead,
And the cities said to me: "Why are you dying?
We are satisfied, if you are; but why did I die?"

—RANDALL JARRELL, "Losses"

A gnome-shaped white-haired man
touched me on the shoulder.

I started from my trance.

He beckoned with his finger
as in a fairy tale.

I followed him down palace halls
until he unlocked a simple door.

The Royal Throne Room,
inlaid with mother-of-pearl, shimmered.

His dark eyes shone as he showed
the silver floors

woven peacock feathers on the walls,
golden Buddhas their legs smooth from touching.

He said across the dark,
"My family has guarded these treasures
for generations. What will happen?

Many of my people will die.
My country will die."

He looked to me for help.
Then locked the door.

Sitting in a lounge chair by the pool,
the wife of a TV correspondent said,
"We've just been recalled.
I've got to beat it down

July 4, 1989

liers
ist

Erma
BOMBECK

you. Don't look for dis-
ng in the breeze or pa-
their wings. There are
to gently soothe you.
. . names of people who
me back.

laybe trying to believe
of the painful journey,
op and force yourself to
u have resisted. There
ir as you acknowledge
he beginning: This is
out. The anger is next
rticular, but only at the
l.

out and touch a name.
name it is. It is no long-
tant. This name had a
and a reason to live. It

vorld are paying an ex-

orbitant price as they struggle toward their
July 4. From South Africa and Northern Ire-
land to the Mideast and Tiananmen Square.
For hundreds of years it has been so. Memori-
als to these battles dot every single country
throughout the world.

I've seen scores of these tributes. The bas
relief map on the ceiling of a cave in Raboul in
the South Pacific honoring the Japanese who
died there. The grand circle of pillars in Belgi-
um honoring every state in our union who sent
young men to die for their cause. The terraced
field in Korea studded with flags and sculp-
tures.

Maybe wars wouldn't be so easy to start if
walls were erected with one simple tribute:
names of men and women who were but are no
more, and will never be again.

*Erma Bombeck is a nationally syndicated co-
lumnist.*

HANDMADE IN LAOS

Outside the hotel in Vientiane
I bought an embroidered bag
from an old mountain woman.

Her brown curled hands
had sewed a thousand perfect stitches
on strips of pink and black appliqué.

From the bottom hung plastic beads,
French coins
République Française 1937
Indochine, they read.

Liberty sits draped on Her throne
a torch in Her hand
a crown on Her silver head.

I felt the mountain lady's presence
as, teeth clenched, I smiled
through diplomatic receptions
my new bag jangling at my side.

What would her people find
to sew on when my country left?
What would they weave
into the tree-of-life design—

film canisters
pop-top rings
rusted casings of M-16's?

OPIUM DENS AND
GOLDEN EGGS

One night we tried an opium den.
There were more than 200 in Vientiane.
The place looked like a hut.
To get there we walked a plank across a ditch.

Dark inside, the addicts lay on mats.
The bare-chested opium man's skin glowed.
The tiny coal of his fire-maker lit one side
of his green face with the raked light of a Caravaggio.

My turn.

I lay beside this stranger
as he heated the sticky brown wax.
Next to me, the brass spittoon
where I'd watched others throwing up.

Inhale cough. Inhale cough.
The pipe went out.
I talked too much
where silence was the rule.

The others wanted theirs.
A French correspondent yelled *shut up*.
Two woman rolled together.
I could hardly walk the plank to leave.

Afraid, I lay awake all night
in a strange hotel room
listening to the rain
feeling my veins tighten around my blood.

Next morning
temples greased in Tiger Balm
we were the only round-eyes
on the plane to Saigon.

      The Plain of Jars.
      It could be Mars.

      The Plain of Jars.
      It could be Mars

stuck in my head
like a record going round and round
like my own blood through my body
the night before.

Then through the crack in the seats ahead of us
I thought I saw a woman as thin as bamboo
slipping Elizabeth Arden lipsticks
and solid-gold eggs to other Asians.

Golden eggs.

In the opium afterhaze
I saw the yellow spun-sugar eggs
left by the Easter bunny
at the foot of my bed.

I remember holding them up to my eye
and through the magic window seeing
tiny bunnies on their hind legs
pushing wheelbarrows filled with colored eggs
across a bright green lawn.

The Plain of Jars.
It could be ours.

The woman's cohorts went to the bathroom
returning with nothing.
I poked my husband and whispered
"We're in the middle of a smuggling ring."

"Where do you suppose they're putting them?"
"Three guesses," he said.

The Queen of Hearts.
She stole some tarts.

The Plain of Mars.
The Plain of Jars.

We reported the racket to customs
but no one was ever caught.
"The goose that laid the golden egg,"
my husband said.

BACK TO
SAIGON

LETTER TO MY SISTER
IN WASHINGTON, D.C.

Saigon

Dear Sis,

Janie, the weather person on the Armed Services Station, is showing 95° in Danang, snow falling in Washington, and I'm sitting here thinking of you and wondering how a Thomas's English muffin tastes in the morning.

I'd give anything to be cold. Sometimes when I wake up in the middle of the night, I go to the kitchen, open the refrigerator door and just stand there in my nightgown letting the cool air hit my skin.

I wish I were there. We could take a walk. Old Dusty could pull us around Cleveland Park on her red leash. The huge oaks up by the Washington Cathedral would be weighted down with snow.

Afterwards, we'd sit around your kitchen table, drinking coffee, watching "General Hospital" and gossiping about everything as fast as we could. I'm so t i r e d of speaking s l o w l y.

Yesterday on my way to the market, I was walking along like a true colonialist in my straw hat, when a cyclo man jumped on my back. I don't know why I didn't buckle to the pavement—but those cyclo men smoke so much opium they weigh nothing. His egret legs wrapped around my waist as he pounded on me yelling, "Get out. Get out. Get out of my country."

I can't blame him. "Troi oi." We say this all the time. Literally, it means "Oh Heaven," but I think it means "It's all too much." No doubt it loses something in translation. Sometimes I think I'm losing something in translation.

Write to me—anything—from home. How's Ali MacGraw's mustache?

Troi-oi
Wendell

TAPES

When the bigwigs flew out from New York
to interview President Thieu,
my husband was allowed to sit in.

The cassette he brought to the palace
had Bob Dylan singing on it.

When the tape was transcribed
we heard Dylan wailing in the background,
"Hey, Mr. Tambourine Man, play a song for me"

as Thieu droned on
about progress in Vietnamization,
assurances of his landslide victory.

VICTORY

After President Thieu won the election
by 99.4% of the vote,
we crowned him "Ivory Snow"
99^{44}/$_{100}$% pure.

JOHNNIE WALKER
TO THE RESCUE

President Thieu had an aide
who spoke perfect English
wore a baseball cap.

When he had the press to dinner
he had the menu printed on the table
so we knew what we were eating:

hedgehog
duck's feet
crisp baby sparrows from the nest.

I gagged down the first duck's foot
with Scotch.
He saw and ordered me another.

GI JOE

One afternoon three GI's came to my balcony.
The blond, from Iowa City, looked like Gary Cooper.
I told him I had a boyfriend once
who went to college in Des Moines.

It was exciting just to say the names.

I told him I raised a black Angus heifer for 4-H.
Never could train her either.
She pulled me through the sawdust
at the fairgrounds in Santa Ynez, California.

I won a red ribbon.
We laughed about ribbons hanging in barns
all across America.
He talked about his high school basketball team

and in the same breath
asked if I minded his smoking heroin.
As he tapped white powder onto a Kool cigarette,
I expected to see the Man with the Golden Arm.

Instead he kept on talking about home
said he started smoking the Big H
the first day in the Nam,
the smell of marijuana was too easy to detect.

SOLDIER'S GRAFFITO

"I think I'm falling in love
with my right hand."

DUNCAN'S HORSES

I taught the Elizabethan concept of order in *Macbeth*,
The Great Chain of Being,
every speck of creation a link in nature's chain.
When disorder erupts, the links break
moving along the chain in a ripple movement.

When Macbeth murders Duncan
night strangles day
mousing owls kill falcons
Duncan's horses break from their stalls
and eat each other.

I taught this theory to Vietnamese teachers
while we defoliated their land
napalmed their children
burned their villages to save them.

Black powder	*Thuốc súng đen*
Blank ammunition	*Đạn thuốc không*
Blasting effect	*Hiệu-lực hơi thổi*
Booster	*Kíp nổ*
Bursting charge	*Thuốc nổ phá*
Bursting effect	*Hiệu-lực phá vỡ*
Coarse grained powder	*Thuốc súng hột to*
Chlorated powder	*Thuốc súng cờ-lo-rát*
Colloidal powder	*Thuốc súng keo*
Complete round	*Phát đạn đầy đủ*
Concrete-piercing shell	*Trái đạn xuyên phá bê-tông*
Delayed action fuze	*Đầu nổ chậm*
Detonator	*Kíp nổ*
Dummy ammunition	*Đạn giả*
Fine grained powder	*Thuốc súng hột nhỏ*
Fulminating powder	*Thuốc súng fu-mi-nát*
Gas shell	*Trái đạn hơi độc*
Graze burst shell	*Trái đạn chạm nổ*
Gun cotton	*Bông thuốc súng*
High explosive powder	*Thuốc nổ phá*
High explosive shell	*Trái đạn nổ phá*
Illuminating shell	*Trái đạn chiếu sáng*
Incendiary shell	*Trái đạn lửa*
Increment	*Thuốc bồi*
Instantaneous fuze	*Đầu nổ tức khắc*
Live ammunition	*Đạn thật*
Lacrymatory shell	*Trái đạn cay mắt*
Mechanical fuze	*Đầu nổ cơ-vận*
Mercury fulminate	*Ful-mi-nát, thủy-ngân*
Nitrocotton	*Bông thuốc súng*
Nitrogen powder	*Thuốc đạm-tố*

Piercing effect	*Hiệu-lực xuyên phá*
Powder bag	*Túi thuốc nạp*
Primer mixture	*Thành phần thuốc nổ*
Propelling charge	*Thuốc tống*
Proximity fuze	*Đầu nổ sóng điện*
Quick burning powder	*Thuốc súng nhạy*
Rocket	*Hỏa-tiễn*
Safety pin	*Chốt an-toàn*
Saltpeter	*Hỏa-tiêu*
Shape charge	*Thuốc nổ lõm*
Shell	*Trái đạn*
Shrapnel shell	*Trái đạn ghém*
Smoke shell	*Trái đạn khói*
Smokeless powder	*Thuốc súng không khói*
Sympathetic detonation	*Nổ vì giao-cảm*
The base	*Đuôi đạn*
The body	*Thân đạn*
The case	*Vỏ đạn*
The fuze	*Đầu nổ*
The primer	*Hạt nổ*
The rotating band	*Đai đạn*
Time fuze	*Đầu nổ cao*
T and P (Time and Percussion) fuze	*Đầu nổ lưỡng tính*
To set a fuze	*Điều-chỉnh đầu nổ*
Trinitrotoluene T. N. T.	*Thuốc nổ TNT*
Training ammunition	*Đạn huấn-luyện*

INVASION

The morning of the Laotian invasion
I got up with my husband at dawn
took his picture on the balcony.
He looked small and pale
wrapped in an army-issue camouflage poncho
we kept on the bed.
The press was forbidden to file stories home.
There was even an embargo on the embargo.

When his friend came to tell me
that the first helicopter had gone down
that everyone on it was dead
that the pilots were Vietnamese
that they flew north into enemy fire
that my husband was on the second and O.K.
I wanted to sleep with this messenger.

Instead, we stayed up
smoking strong grass
listening to Sweet Baby James

> *I've seen fire and I've seen rain*
> *I've seen sunny days that I thought would never end*
> *I've seen lonely times when I could not find a friend*
> *but I always thought that I'd see you again . . .*

The music burned in
                    dodged
scored along my nerves
new, three-dimensional
guitar   notes   words
cascading over each other
rising like the heat
held there.

VIETNAMIZATION

The name of the operation
was changed
from Dewey Canyon II
to Lam Son 719.

EDITOR

In his air-conditioned room
24 floors above the Avenue of the Americas
the editor waits for the story.

He tells his researcher,
"I've heard from my Pentagon division.
Now I'm waiting for my flower children in Saigon."

LETTER FROM A SOLDIER

Five flights below me
the landlady's daughter
received a letter
from her fiancé fighting in Laos.

"We are running scared. We cannot hold the line. Everyone is running.
No one even stops to dig in. We call in American support. Nothing
happens. I doubt that I will make it home."

I heard about the letter
told her my husband
was doing a story
on the invasion of Laos.

When I asked if he could quote from her letter,
she took the paper from her pocket
and burned it on the table
with a look beyond disgust.

GECKOS

Evenings, waiting for you
I watched pale geckos
belly their way
across my ceiling.

Slowly three, sometimes five
(their large eyes never blinked)
manoeuvered to surround
a fluttering moth.

After hours of upside-down stalking,
by some signal I never saw,
one would uncurl his thin tongue
and strike! Swallow the insect whole.

This happened every night in silence.

It was strange how at the end
I looked forward to the geckos' coming out.

THE AMERICAN ADVISER

We met an American adviser
in a French café
on the southern coast of Vietnam.
Over a bowl of soupe Chinoise
he told us about his dog.

It seems he raised a large retriever
in his village in the jungle
on vitamins and cases of Alpo
his mother sent from home.

The dog was the wonder of the village.
Children stood in line
to touch his golden hair.

When I asked him what would happen
to the dog when he left,
he said not even the village elders
could afford to feed it.
He would have to shoot it.

EXAMS

During examination week
there was a demonstration
in the more radical
School of Science.

I decided to hold my orals anyway.

I was asking Mr. Phuc
to explain the role of the witches in *Macbeth*
when we heard an explosion
and both dived under my desk.

He pointed to the book in his hand.
Through tear-gassed eyes,
I read the title dimly:
Shakespeare without Tears.

We held on to each other
under my desk
our cheeks wet
with laughing and crying.

REST AND RECREATION

After all the dragon jars
the rows of Buddha smiles

gold leaf plastered
on guard dogs outside temples

after all the burning sandalwood
cobras, firebirds
teacups of the moon palace

I climbed the steps
of a Portuguese church in Macao.

Cut in gray stone
above the door
ox, eagle, lion, and winged man

Matthew, Mark, Luke, and John
I recognized them!

In a French restaurant in Saigon,
I overheard a GI
say to his Vietnamese date,

"You see what I mean?
Why I have to get out?
Back in the world,
they have cabbages *this* big."

He stared through the empty
circle of his arms
at the Brussels sprouts
piled on his plate.

THE NOODLE CART

My friends sent back rain drums from Laos,
lacquered trays with goldfish, ceramic elephants.
Once I knew we were leaving
I wanted a noodle cart

the old kind,
like the one I passed each morning on Le Thanh Ton,
with the stained-glass panels
of dragons and oceans and mythic sword fights.

I loved the giant ladles
the blue-and-white bowls in racks
the pots of boiling soup
over the charcoal braziers
the tiny stools on the street.

I loved the way the vendor
knew his clients
knew their favorite noodles
what they liked on top
like a waitress knowing you like your eggs
"sunny-side up" in an American coffee shop.

I asked Mrs. Nga to help me find a noodle cart.
After a month she said she had.
To buy one, she had to talk a family out of theirs.
The son was all in favor, but not the father
who was dead against selling the family business.

Now the noodle cart stands
on my brother's porch in California
stocked with little green bottles of Perrier water
Mr. and Mrs. T's Bloody Mary Mix.

NEW YORK CITY
1971-1975

PACKERS

When our shipping crate arrived at home,
our cameras, lenses,
tape recorders, cassettes, typewriters
and drip-dry shirts were gone.

In our living room I stared at a black X
inked on the outside of the half-empty box.
Above it, a hole, axed in the plywood
stared back like a skull.

The men who'd worked three days
in our Saigon apartment
wrapping our possessions
carefully in newspaper

put all the black market stuff
in one place and marked it
so that their cohorts at the docks
would know just where to go in
and scoop it out.

LETTER FROM A FRIEND
STILL IN SAIGON

Dear Wendy,

In answer to your question, I've had it here. If I come around the corner one more time to see a cyclo driver pissing on the sidewalk or if the god-awful smell of frying nuoc mam wafts through the window one more breakfast, I'll throw up on the whole village of people parked outside my walls.

Everyone we knew and loved in the press corps has moved on. We are stuck here one more year.

We are in a new villa since you left. The cook took everything that was not nailed down except a mutt we did not want and the lawn.

Papayas are coming into season. The strawberries from Dalat are here. Otherwise, you can have this Pearl of the Orient.

This will have to be short. We're going to Hong Kong in two days for R&R. I can't wait to call Mandarin room service from the bathtub then jump into those pressed linen sheets.

Otherwise, you're lucky to be back in the world of round-eyes and Rexall Drugs.

Miss you,

Susan

REUNION

Late January. Tet.
It's been four years.
Mrs. Nga is coming toward me
on the Avenue of the Americas.
The Christmas decorations are down
in New York City
where buildings slice the sky
streets smoke from underneath
doors open automatically.

She's wearing a red nylon ski parka.
She looks small and alone
beside all the reflecting glass.
I remember my first walk in Saigon
asking everyone I met for directions
to Na Goo Yen Huey Street.
I was on it. Nguyen Hue
pronounced *When Way*.

It's snowing.
Vietnamese fear the cold.
When I was living there,
I dreamt of snow
dreamt of diving into a river of crystals
like an otter on a slide
covering myself from head to toe
in soft white powder.

Inside a restaurant, snowflakes melt
on the smooth red surface of her coat.
"From the rummage sale," she says
hanging it on a hook.

For some reason, I tell her
that as Saigon fell, the coded message
played on the U.S. radio
for Americans to go to their evacuation stations
was "the temperature report for Saigon
is 105° and rising"
followed by the first thirty seconds
of "I'm Dreaming of a White Christmas."

She tells me how she managed to escape
four days before the Americans,
how she misses her country, her mother,
how the church helped her find a house in Greenwich.
She says now it is she who has a problem.
Her son has fallen in love
with the daughter of their American tutor.

They stay upstairs in his room all day
playing loud music, will not be part of the family
not even to come down to dinner.
"Troi oi," I sigh and she laughs.
Remembering her advice to me in Vietnam,
I say "give me a week"
hoping I'll come up with something
to bring peace to her American household.

NGA'S
STORY

KUNMING
HANOI
YEN BAI
HADONG
1927-1940

THE SCROLL

My father owned a Chinese scroll
big as a wall
nine different birds
painted on silk
some flying, some standing
some building nests.
He named all of us,
six boys and three girls,
after the birds in the scroll.

Phuong for phoenix
Nhan for skylark
Hac for heron
Bang for eagle
Cau for dove
Nga for swan
Hai for seagull
and later
Yen for swallow
Tuoc for robin.

Whenever we moved
he rolled it up himself
carried it on his shoulders
from one place to another
even when the silk had faded yellow.

LEAVING CHINA

I was born in China in 1927.
My father was sent there to teach.
He graduated with honors from the University of Hanoi,
should have been allowed to choose his post,
but his French superior wanted a bribe.

My father was honest
influenced too much by Confucius.
When he refused to give money, he was sent to Kunming
a province on the border of Vietnam.
He always said it was a punishment.

I remember the day we left China for Hanoi.
I was the youngest in the family then.
The whole town came to say goodbye to my father.
His students lit firecrackers
hung flowers from the train.

My mother's friends cried.
She lay down in the dark
all the way to Hanoi.
The train burned charcoal.
When I stuck my head out the window
dust blew in my eyes.

RIDING WITH MY FATHER

I remember the days
in the waterfall highlands
riding through the jungle
in front of my father's saddle
feeling his arms around me.
Together we'd cross mountain passes:
wild orchids in the morning mist
chattering monkeys
pythons sunning on the rocks.
Below us, transparent streams
where the soldiers, our escorts,
would stop to catch tiny striped fish
in their hands.

I'd carry them in the cold pool
of a wrapped banana leaf
watching the water move from side to side.
When I was scared, I'd cover my eyes.
At the steepest places, he'd dismount
and lift me on his shoulders
leading his brown horse
over the narrow mountain passes
going to inspect the schools
in Yen Bai.

Few of the fish
ever reached home alive.

MY FATHER'S TREASURES

Each time my father gambled with his boss,
the Province Chief,
I was to bring the silver betel box.
In it were betel, lime, the bitter bark of a tree,
tobacco and two sweet-smelling flowers from our garden.
My parents encouraged us to try it
said the lime would make our teeth strong.
They chewed, then spat red juice
into a brass pot polished bright each day.

My father stored his medicines in wooden boxes—
white cinnamon, dark cinnamon, ginseng root.
One day he brought home a python.
He kept its bile sac in a jar of alcohol.
After several weeks, he took it out
and dried it in the sun.
When we were sick,
he smashed the dried bile into little pieces
making us swallow the bitter medicine.
Sometimes he sucked strength
from young deer antlers
throwing his head back like a giant.
Deer antlers, he said, would give you many children.

Each morning before school
my job was to polish the antiques
kept in a drawer in the lacquer chest.
My father was afraid of being poisoned.
He always carried his special chopsticks
on his trips to the countryside.
They were black with silver tips.
A mountain chief gave them to him

promising that the tips would change color
if there was poison.

I was never sure whom he thought would kill him,
the French or the Vietnamese.

VISITING MY AUNTIE LAN

My father and I visited my auntie in Vinh Yen.
The cyclo man ran rhythmically
through the immense flat fields
of rice and corn—all yellowing.
Wind blew through the rice like waves.

Young girls cut the rice with their long scythes
piling it up
singing ritual folksongs
of the landscape to their sweethearts.

First the girls sang:

> *Can you guess how many rice plants we have?*
> *Do you know how many tributaries the river has?*
> *Who can sweep all the leaves in the forest?*

Then the boys would call back:

> *Before I answer you,*
> *you answer me.*

> *In how many years will the moon be old?*
> *How many years before we can say*
> *the mountain is old enough to stay forever?*

They would tease:

> *Oh young miss with the bucket on your shoulder*
> *could you please give me a bucket*
> *to water my evergreen plants?*
> *If the evergreen gets more leaves,*
> *a phoenix can stand on each branch.*

At night my cousins walked me through the rice fields.
The sound of the gongs from the harvest festival got closer and closer.
We watched the boys and girls dance in the moonlight
to the beat of the drums that hung from their necks.

Too excited to sleep
I'd lie awake in the strange bed
listening to the dogs barking in the village.

POLITICS

My father told me that when he was twenty
he taught himself French
so he could make more money
become a big man, a mandarin,
a Minister of Education.
Education, examination, administration:
that was the Confucian way.

We learned French too
like birds who cannot speak a human tongue.
We learned like parrots
and did not understand—
the alphabet, the verbs.

We hated the French
though Father worked with them.
We especially hated their long noses
called them *mui lo*,
which means, the nose looks at the mouth.

We never had them in our houses.
We saw them in the streets
heard they would rape and torture us
put electric strings on our fingers.
The most savage were the Algerians.
We named them *red gullets*.
When they killed you,
they ripped your belly out.

I never understood politics.
In the highlands Father warned us
not to take any leaflets.
They were guerrilla propaganda

would ruin our family's name.
His look scared us into silence.

Actually, many people entered our house at night.
They never went out in the day.
They talked quietly,
left in the black of night.
When I asked Father, he said
they were my aunties and uncles.
I wondered why I had so many.

THE EXECUTION

My elder brother remembers the day of the execution
in Yen Bai when I was very young.
Everyone in the house got up so early
it was still dark outside.

Father was serious.
He had received an invitation
from the French to watch an execution.
The French cut the throats of thirteen people
with a big machine—a guillotine.

The roads were blocked for miles.
There was no school.
I was not allowed to go.
The sky was dark and gloomy
the mountain covered with clouds.

My brother escaped from the house to watch.
When he came home,
he dared not sleep alone.
Father was very pale.

Years later, I understood
they had killed Nguyen Thai Hoc
and his sweetheart, Co Giang
and her sister, Co Bac—
national heroes and heroines
who fought against the French.

When he spoke of the highlands,
my father said,
"Difficult geography makes heroes."

SON NU—MOUNTAIN GIRLS

My elder sister
will remember
happier mornings
in the highlands.
Awake
before school
we'd look
through the window
up at the blue mountain
see the girls
in their long
navy blue skirts
their embroidered vests
big straw baskets
on their heads,
weaving their way
single file
slowly
down the path
covered with dew
in the coming sunlight.

We'd race from the house
to buy the sweet sim fruit
which turned our tongues purple.

OUR HOUSE IN HADONG

Our best house, the house where we were happy,
was our brick house on Ha Van Street
with its two hectares of land
lichee and mangosteen and starfruit in the back,
the two Hoa Moc trees white as snow in the front.
We'd put the petals in our tea to sweeten our breath.

From far down the road
I could smell the heavy jackfruit.
Father never allowed us to eat them
said they were too rich for the climate.
He'd give them to the soldiers outside the walls.
When he was away, we ate until we got fevers.
My younger sister climbed the apple trees
and shook the apples down.

We had everything.
There was a flower garden
with dark red roses, orchids and yellow mimosa.
We had our own cauliflower, tomatoes,
the artichokes my father loved,
chickens, pigs, ducks and pigeons.
We needed the market only for beef
and rice kept in giant brown jars in the storeroom.

We even had two ponds.
Each New Year
we'd let the water out of the big pond
to catch the butterfish
we'd fed all year.

On a tiny island in the middle of the smaller pond,
the cook built an imitation mountain

with caves, bamboo, porcelain angels,
and two old matchmakers playing chess.
When the moon came up,
we'd watch the goldfish move in the warm water
and listen to night noises
remembering the sounds of the jungle.

MY MOTHER

My mother always dressed with care.
She'd wrap her long black hair
into a black velvet turban
secured with a long gold pin.
She wore gold earrings
and a necklace of 1,000 fine gold beads.
(We'd count them round her neck.)
Embroidered in red beads
on her tiny velvet shoes
were her name and my father's.

As a child, her mother
encouraged her to dye her teeth black—
a sign of wealth and beauty.
My father dyed his, too.
When he became more westernized,
he wanted his white teeth back.
He went to bed
with a special leaf in his mouth,
but he never could get rid of the black.
His teeth remained a strange in-between color.

Each afternoon Mother would go gambling
with the Province Chief's wife
as was the duty of a mandarin's wife.
She'd be introduced as Ba Doc Hoc,
wife of the Minister of Education,
or as Ba Lon, Big Lady.

I watched from the window
as she settled in the rickshaw
first straightening the long skirt of her brown ao dai
over the pale pink one underneath.

Then the rickshaw man
would hand her the umbrella
with the gold handle
and out the gate they'd go.

THE FOUR DEMEANORS

When she was home, my mother instructed
my sister and myself in the four demeanors
as her mother had instructed her,
believing a woman should sacrifice for her husband.

Cong—manage the household within the budget
          including cooking, sewing, knitting, care
          of the husband, education of the children
          all to save the husband's face

Dung—maintain an attractive and cheerful appearance
          most particularly for the husband
          (She showed us how to fix our hair, keep
           our bodies clean.)

Ngon—speak properly, never raise one's voice
          in front of the servants or other family
          members

Hanh—know one's place
          show respect and gratitude for parents and elders
          faithfulness and sacrifice for the husband

She knew parts of the "Warrior's Wife" by heart
and made us learn it
to show how a brave wife behaves
when her husband goes to war to serve his country.

from "THE LAMENT OF THE WARRIOR'S WIFE"

Dang Tran Con (18th century)

The farewell cup is not empty, but you shake your sword;
Spear lowered, you point at the den of wild beasts.
Like Chieh-tzu, who fought the Lou-lan,
Like the Conqueror of Waves who held down the Man-chu,
Like them, you say, so you.
Red: your coat is as red as cinnabar,
White: Your horse is as white as new snow,
His bells begin to shake in time to the drums.
We stood facing each other. Now you are gone.
When I see the bridge I will see our parting.
I stand alone on the road, sadly watching your banners flutter away.
The first chariots draw near Chi-liao
But the cavalry to the rear is still wandering through
   the Ch'ang-yang valley

                                    . . .

This confinement is my destiny—
But who has decreed that you remain so far away?
I expected to live with you like a fish in water:
How could I know we were to be as separate as water and clouds?
I had no dream of being a warrior's wife,
Nor did you expect to be forever away.
Why must we be apart
And lonely in the morning, in the night?
We were young, we lived elegantly and well
in our happy marriage.
Who could bear to separate such lovers?
Now days warm you, nights chill you,
But there are mountains between us.
When you left there were no orioles in the willow trees.
You told me you would return with the cuckoos.
The cuckoos have come, the orioles have gone,

And there are swallows warbling in front of the house.
When you left the plum trees had felt no cold winds.
You told me you would return when the peach tree blooms.
Winter had blown on the peach trees,
Along the river the rose mallows are all withered.
You told me to wait on Lung-hsi hill,
And I waited from early dawn, and saw no one:
Only dry leaves fluttered down on my hairpin.

. . .

MY GRANDMOTHER

My mother missed her mother so much
she convinced my father to let her live with us.
We loved her and held her in respect.

Before we had electric heat,
my mother ordered one of us to lie
in Grandmother's bed to warm it up for her.

Grandmother would instruct us daily, especially the girls.

    "Be khong vin ca gay canh"
    A young branch must be put into shape
    lest it break when it's old.

    Girls, do not hang your underwear
    on a man's door.
    If your father or your brother pass under it,
    he will have bad luck.

    On your wedding day, your guests will chew the betel.
    If the color runs red, you will have great happiness.
    If not, your guests will be silent and worry for you.

    Remember.
    Once you go to your husband's house,
    you must wait on everyone,
    even the dog.

We had few toys, no radio.
We would sit on her lap
listening to her stories.

GRANDMOTHER'S FABLE

Once upon a time there lived a farming family.
The mother died, leaving three sons
to live with their father.
When the father became ill
and thought he was going to die,
he called his children to his bedside
and handed each of them
a large bunch of chopsticks tied together.

He said, "Whoever can break this,
I will reward."
Not one was able to.

The father then handed each of them
only one set.
This they broke easily.
The father said, "If you remain united,
no one can harm you,
but if you separate, then you will be hurt.
This is the advice I leave with you.
The heritage I have for you
is in the rice fields."

After the father's death,
the three brothers stayed together
even after they married.
They did not find any golden treasures
buried in the rice fields.
They plowed and planted
and the ground gave successful harvests.
They realized working together
and working hard were life's riches.

OUR RICKSHAW MAN

Anh Nhi was our rickshaw man.
"Anh" means brother.
He wore a cone-shaped straw hat
tied under his chin.
His smooth legs were wrapped
in red ribbons.
I never told my mother,
but I liked his fluffy rice
better than the finer rice
up at the big house.

He was loyal to our family,
but gambling was his weakness.
Sometimes he'd disappear for a week.
He'd come back so tired,
he would sleep under the high bed
with the legs carved to look like dragons,
afraid my mother would find him.

MY NURSE

My vu em
who nursed me from her breasts
stayed with our family most of her life
after her own baby died.
Even when I grew up,
she'd come and meet me at the gate
just as she did in the old days.
Nothing had changed—
not the smell
not the dress
not the sweets she hid under her waistband.

One night I heard my mother scream
and all the lights came on.
I asked my vu em what was happening
and she said mother was having a baby.
I saw my father running in and out
asking for hot water, more towels.
I ran to ask my sister where babies came from.
She told me from Mother's armpit.
I ran around the house telling everyone,
"Mother's having a baby from her armpit."

My vu em terrified me
with stories of the phantom
who lived in the Hoa Dai tree
and would stand at the head of my bed,
where I slept with my sister,
sticking its tongue,
as red as blood, out at us,
threatening to curl around my legs

and squeeze me to death
unless I slept.

I was old before I dared to sleep alone
and would run by any Hoa Dai tree.

ELEVEN YEARS OLD

My mother said I was growing up.
I looked at myself in the mirror
and I knew I was.
My eyes were big and brown
my cheeks very pink.
I smiled all the time.
My brothers would pinch me
saying "come on, daughter-in-law."
I did not understand
and would run into my room.

I began to like music,
reading poems and novels.
My third brother had a huge collection.
I loved *les livres roses*,
a series for children,
especially one about the vengeance of snakes,
one where the students go to fairyland
and *Tam Cam*, our *Cinderella*,
about the real sister and the stepsister and the prince.
I was a dreamer.

MY ELDEST BROTHER, PHUONG

I remember the day my eldest brother left,
the first separation in the family.
My parents rented a car
and took him to boarding school.
There was no high school where we lived.
Each night I passed his room, I cried.

He was the one who taught me to sing.
The one who lost his lover to his best friend
and put his sadness in his songs.
The one who knew when I was sad
watching the sun set behind the blue mountains,
happy when the morning sunshine
lit the tops of trees.

I knew my father would beat me for singing.
     "Singing is doing nothing.
     Nice girls from good families do not sing."
We met in secret.
     "Brothers and sisters must not sit together.
     Brothers and sisters must sit far from each other
     unless accompanied."

After school, I'd take a bath
change my clothes,
pretend to be visiting a friend
next door across the wall.
Instead, I'd run to my brother
waiting for me with his guitar
at the far end of the yard
in the summer thatch house
under the cool palm-leaf roof.

MY BROTHER'S STORY
OF *Quynh Hoa,*
THE PRINCESS FLOWER

This princess was so lovely
her own brother fell in love with her.
Because of his lust,
she felt she was no longer a virgin
and that he had sinned
against their ancestors.
She asked their forgiveness
then killed herself.

A mysterious flower
grew from the spot where she died.
The flower bloomed at night,
but never when her brother was there
though he sent special guards to tend it.
She wished to punish her brother
show the kingdom
she was still a virgin.

The first time our princess flower bloomed
we invited our friends to the courtyard
by the imitation mountain.
We circled the flower
with its fragile cream and pink blossoms,
played our guitars and sang,
watching its petals come out
little by little in the moonlight.

THE SCHOOL PLAY

One of our best-kept secrets
was that I was the head angel in the school play
and Father did not know it,
though he was head of the education board.

Everyone in the area came,
even the Province Chief.
When the curtain was raised
on the beautiful landscape
there stood twenty angels,
all dressed in white
with white flowers in their long black hair.

We sang the story of a romantic king
who journeyed out with these maidens
to go sightseeing.
Since he was a human king,
he drank too much wine.
Enchanted by the moonlight,
he journeyed to the heavens.
I was the angel who showed him the way back.

My eldest brother was the head of the orchestra.
My second played the flute,
my third the Spanish guitar.

At the end we sang farewell
to the king, played by our teacher.
Everyone clapped warmly.
As he walked off,
his crown slipped from his head
he tripped on his robe
and fell from the stage.

I stood there laughing
until I saw my father
give the signal to pull down the curtain.

That afternoon a soldier came to summon Father
to the Province Chief's house.
I watched him leave the yard.
He wore the long black topcoat
Mother had given him
with the blue brocade one underneath.
From the collar hung an ivory nameplate
engraved with his position in red characters.
I knew the summons was my fault.
I had caused my family ridicule
and ran to my brother for protection.

That evening we were all called to the table.
We invited our parents to eat first,
as is our custom.
My father took his chopsticks in his long fingers.
He looked at me with a little smile
and said to my mother,
"From now on, you will have the driver
take Nga in the afternoons
to the Province Chief's house
to teach his children music."
My eyes shone as I looked at my brother.

MATCHMAKERS

We had a formal relationship with our mother.
We never sat next to her,
but stood behind her chair.
Her days were filled with social obligations,
gambling with the Big Boss's wife.
Hour after hour they played *To Tom*,
a Vietnamese game for five players
120 pieces of red and black characters.

As they played, the women discussed
their children's fate.
"My son is so good at school,
he will become a mandarin."
"My daughter is so capable,
she runs the house without me."
Sometimes a real matchmaker would join in
praising her latest bride-to-be.

Even in my day, we did not pick our own husbands.
That was our parent's choice.
Once married, your fate was sealed.
You could not return to your home.
Everyone would think you had been rejected for a reason.
This would bring shame to your family.

TO THE EMPEROR

Once every three years in the spring,
my father would go to Hue, the ancient capital,
to pay homage to the Emperor Bao Dai.

My mother explained
this was the Nam Giao ceremony.
The Emperor was the Son of Heaven.

He communicated with the Universe
asking for blessings for his people.
The mandarins assisting him at court

were not allowed to look at him.
This was a sign of disrespect
in the old days punishable by death.

My mother brought down a special box
from its high place
unpacked father's deep blue brocade robe.

The soldiers warmed the heavy iron
in a clay oven filled with charcoal,
handed it to my mother.

As she smoothed the folds of the robe,
I stared at its embroidered double herons.
My job was to dust my father's black cloth boots.

KHAM THIEN,
THE STREET OF THE TEA HOUSES

There was a street called Kham Thien
between Hanoi and Hadong.
We were forbidden to go there
forbidden to even mention the name.
This was the street of the tea houses.
A senior geisha trained the younger geishas
to entertain the guests, only men.
They would play games
sing poems to the beat of a drum
My father loved the music.
He would go to these places often with Mr. van Phuc.

One day my mother said,
"Didn't you know your daddy had a friend
who was not a good friend?
Mr. van Phuc knew that your father was generous
that he had money.
Mr. van Phuc did not.
He spent days and days on the Kham Thien road
looking for the geisha who was the best singer
and reported back to your father."

Mother knew that if that man came to our house
Father would dress and leave in five minutes.
She tried to stop him, but it was no use.
He said he would only go for a little while
but he would always go for the whole night
and come home in the morning.
I hated that man.
One day when I saw him at the door
instead of asking him into the sitting room

and telling my father
I turned my head and went into my own room.

One night when Father came home late
I heard my mother's voice talking loudly.
Each one yelled at the other
and then my mother started to cry.
Father left the bedroom and slept on the couch.
The next morning when Father went out,
Mother ordered Anh Nhi, the rickshaw man,
to follow without letting Father know.

She told me and my sister to come with her
saying, "Hurry. Hurry, we have important work to do."
The three of us sat in the rickshaw
following close behind my father.
My mother said nothing.
Her face looked sad.

After one half hour we reached the country.
On either side were fields of rice
turning yellow and smelling so sweet.
Each time the breeze blew
the rice bent its head
like a wave on the river.
Birds flew here and there over the fields.
I spent my time daydreaming
wondering if I had time to run
deep into the fields picking up the ripe rice
to bring home to burn in our ovens.

Suddenly the rickshaw man stopped
at a row of houses.

There was one very tiny house.
Outside the white door was a fence and bushes of roses.
My mother hurried up to the house
followed by my sister and myself.
She knocked urgently on the door,
but no one answered.
Finally she pushed the door with all her strength
opening it onto a bed
a small sitting room and a closet.

When she saw my father's clothes in the closet,
she began to tremble.
She took the clothes from the hanger
then turned and ran from the house
seizing my hand
as we ran down the street after the lady
who had escaped from her house.
My mother cried over and over
"Oh, how selfish man is. How savage."
When we came close to the lady,
my mother stood in front of her and cried.
My sister said something and shook her head.
I was a machine following my mother and sister.

When we got home, Father was waiting for us
in his favorite chair.
His face was very very angry.
He said my mother was a big lady.
Why should she go running after another lady?
He said he was ashamed to have such a wife.
She said she had not meant to behave in such a way
but since my father was showing his unfaithfulness

she had to protect her happiness.
They were both talking and the noise got louder and louder.

When my brother came from his room,
all was silent.
We did not go to school.
There was sadness in the atmosphere of our family.

MY ELDER SISTER

Nhan was six years older than me.
I cried when she first went to school
leaving me alone at home.
She left school at fourteen.
Father did not believe in education for women.
It is our tradition that the eldest girl
learns to care for the house and the children
to prepare to become a good wife herself.

My mother turned over all powers to her.
She took care of the house money, made our clothes,
planned and cooked our meals.
She practiced French embroidery
and even took French cooking lessons,
a sign of status in the provinces.
My father thought no one was good enough for her.
She wore a white silk suit
with flowers embroidered on the cuffs.

She was strict
would beat us, even my brothers,
with a rattan rope.
I was beaten for being late,
and once for spilling violet ink on my clothes.
We did not have ballpoint pens.
We carried our own ink to school
in little glass bottles.

LOVE LETTERS

Sister and I slept in the same bed.
In the summer when it was hot,
we slept on polished boards with no sheets.
I was still afraid of the phantom.
Knowing this, my sister threatened
not to sleep with me
unless I delivered letters to her boyfriends.

Sometimes, I would deliver them.
Other times, embarrassed near boys,
I'd drop them down a hole
in between the bricks that covered the ditch
at the back of the house.
I'd watch the dark water carry them away.

When I was 12 and she was 18,
my father caught me with a letter.
He took it from me,
then beat us till we both bled.
Gradually, I came to understand
he wanted to stop us from loving the wrong person,
a person who would not be approved by the family.

In our country a girl should be pure
when she marries.
The purer she is
the more she is worth.
A big wedding means much face.
Parents raise their daughters
many years for that day.

AUNTIE LAN'S SON

Auntie Lan sent her tiny quiet son
from the countryside to live with us
to be educated by my father up to university.

When he was five years old,
she came to take him home
to marry a woman twenty-two years old.

She said her husband needed another strong woman
to work in his rice fields.
My father could not change her mind.

At the wedding the bride held her husband
in her arms. After the ceremony,
she gave him a bath.

The peasants joke about such marriages:

A husband and wife are walking in a field.
They come to a ditch.
The wife jumps over easily,
but the tiny husband falls in.
The water is high and rushing.
She calls out,
"Friend, come help me.
Lend me a bucket
to scoop up my husband."

FOLK POEM
OF THE MISMATCHED BRIDE

You love money so much
you would marry a little boy.
In the upper village
in the lower village
count the men.
Why bring your body to a little boy?
Can he massage your breasts?
In the wintertime
the boy tries to warm himself
by lying near you
and you must cover him.
Nine out of ten nights
you sleep alone.

I cannot tell anyone of my situation.
My youth is wasted,
my cheeks no longer rosy
all because of a tiny boy.
In the middle of the night
I rub him
waste my time.
Sad, I try to wake him.
He is too small. It is no use.
He snores gently into the next morning.

Dear Sister,
how many times will the flower blossom?

AUNTIE MAI

My father's younger sister was my favorite.
I wanted to go live with her in Hanoi.
She was westernized
had many French friends
who came to her house.
When she came to our house
she and father whispered in his room.
Once we did not see her for three months.
Father said she was busy.

Later he told me
she traveled in disguise all over Vietnam
as a nun, a nurse, a village teacher.
Much later I found out
her house was the headquarters
of the Quoc Dan Dang.
She passed on information
learned from the French.
She was arrested and tortured.
They put wires in her breasts
ants in her lower parts
but she never told them anything.
Eventually, they killed her.

HADONG
KUNMING
HANOI
1940-1954

MEETING BAO IN HADONG

The electric train that took us to school
passed by every fifteen minutes.
We heard the clang and ran to catch it.
Sometimes I stood the whole way,
one brother in front, one in back to protect me.
On the crowded train we met students
from other school levels.
We could tell by the labels on their books.

A man always offered me a seat.
I looked closely at him
though even that was not allowed.
He was handsome, with a high nose and bright eyes.
One morning he asked to borrow my novel.
From then on we began talking about books.
That was our relationship—
his explaining Lamartine to me.

One day he returned my book.
I saw a blue envelope
as sweet-smelling as a flower.
When I read it, my ears grew hot,
my cheeks red and my eyes thrilled.
It was my first love letter.
Then I remembered Father
beating my sister and myself for the letters
I'd carried for her as a go-between.
I hid my letter in the bottom drawer of my desk.

NIGHT-LISTENING

I remember the airplanes coming everyday.
I thought they had come to attack the Japanese
who were everywhere—
in the streets
in the barracks near our house.
We feared them
thought them savage
called them *Chu lun*, midgets.
I trusted the French more than them.
My father stayed home now.

The planes were Allied planes.
My father had shelters dug in the yard
up against the wall under the fruit trees.
They were five meters long
covered over with palm leaves.
When the rains flooded them,
he had concrete ones built.

We learned night-listening
how to tell the heavy bombers
from the inspection planes.

On moonlit nights they'd come.
We'd wake to the alert,
run into the garden
covering our heads.
At first it was so exciting.
We had never seen planes.
Everything seemed so far away
the noise
the shells
the fire.

We'd peek from our shelters
through the trees in the moonlight
to watch the planes shoot shells through the air
in the night sky.
When they'd passed over,
we'd hear the two short whispers of the all-clear sign
and we'd come out
walking past the fish ponds
back to our beds.

VIET MINH

The war between the French and the Viet Minh
came nearer and nearer.
One day, going to school,
I heard an explosion and ran to a ditch
already filled with people.
I lay outside the ditch
watching people run by me
shouting and crying through the smoke.

I did not move until the all-clear signal.
Then I saw people lying on the ground
blood everywhere
hands and legs hanging in a tree.

I yelled and fainted.
When I woke up,
I was in a strange house.
Bao was looking down at me
trying to wipe my face with a handkerchief.

We began to whisper more and more
about arrests.
Many anti-French leaflets
were passed out at school.
Teachers left. My best friend, Dung,
did not come to school.
At first I thought she was sick.
Then I found out she had been arrested.

When friends were arrested,
we were never to speak of that person again.

MUC

One night, caught in the fighting
between the French and the Viet Minh,
we were forced to run.
I was carrying my little brother.
Our dog followed us from house to house, barking.
The neighbors yelled, "Kill him. Kill him.
Otherwise he will get us all killed
with his barking."

My second brother had to shut his eyes
and stab Muc with a knife.
Muc, our trusting dog,
his hair bright and black as velvet.
The look in his eyes
as he opened them wide
just before my brother stabbed him,
so helpless, so pitiful—
it followed me for years.

HIDING AT HOME

The Viet Minh came to power.
Bao Dai was dethroned.
People began to parade by my house.
They sang a special song.
Other people left their houses,
joined in the march.
My sister and I peeked through the gate.

The Province Chief lost his job.
My father lost his.
They'd worked for the French.
Everything stopped for us.
There was no office, no school.
We had no radio.
My younger brother would bring us news
from the street each day.
We stayed home. We had each other.

We stored corn for our animals.
The cook was almost killed on his way to market
for the money he carried.
Nothing was safe.
We heard the Viet Minh buried the French alive.
We were nothing now.
My mother read her Buddhist prayers
over and over.
She would not go to the door.

THE CHINESE

Then the Chinese came to occupy our country,
disarm the Japanese.
We are a small country, but every other country
feels it can treat us like its own home.
Just walk in. Do what you please.

The Chinese frightened me.
Many of them had walked from their country.
Their legs were swollen and festering.
They marched through the streets
in their gray cotton jackets and dirty pants.

Hundreds of them moved to the barracks
near our house where the Japanese had been.
My sister and I climbed the apple tree
to stare down over the wall at them.
When we thought they looked up,
we ducked behind the bricks.

FAMINE

Worse for us than the bombs
was the famine.
We had money,
but there was no rice to buy.
People ate grass.
We read that out in the countryside
peasants were stealing from landlords.
Father told us the French and Japanese
had overstocked rice in the warehouses.
Tons and tons of rotted grain
had to be dumped into the Red River.

When Father tried to fire our servants,
they begged to stay.
They had been loyal.
Where would they go?
How could they eat?
In the end he let them stay
gave them what he could.

When Father had his high position
teachers bought him gifts—
baskets of fruit
lichee and longan.
We stored them in giant vases in the hall,
cut the mooncakes into pieces to be eaten later.
Now he ordered us to eat less rice.
We made rice balls from what we saved
to give to the people outside the walls.

One day when I opened the gate
for Father to go out,
there were corpses collapsed against the wall.

I fainted.
Father offered soldiers money to remove the corpses.
Sometimes they took bodies that were still alive.
People would call from the carts,
"Don't take me. Don't take me.
I'm not dead yet."

INSIDE OUR COURTYARD

I played music in the courtyard
near the imitation mountain
with its caves and its angels
and two matchmakers playing chess.

I played my guitar
at night by the fountain
where carp swam in the pool
and leaves rustled on the bamboo fence.

I sang in the moonlight
smelling the sweet perfume
of the princess flower
carried on the night breeze.

I sang my eldest brother's songs
to express my inside feelings:
"There is a boat floating
with nowhere to land."

Though no one saw me,
I knew they heard my music.
The servants told me the neighbors asked,
"What happened to your second lady last night?"

THE CHINESE GENERAL

We heard a knock one morning.
Father opened the door
and there stood three Chinese officers.
One had so many stars,
I did not know his rank.
"General," my brother whispered.
He was huge, broad-shouldered
with bright eyes that looked straight at you.
My brother and father spoke Chinese.
The general said he heard such sweet music
he followed the sound around the walls
to our front door.
He was surprised to learn
it was a young girl playing the music.
He asked permission to come and listen.
I did not like to play in front of strangers.
Father said I could play in my room
and the general would listen outside the door.

When he wanted to hear me,
I had to dress up and say hello
then return to my room.
He came for several weeks.
I did not understand.
I asked my brother, "Why does he come
and sit outside my room?
Why isn't it boring?"
I felt angry, but could say nothing more
as he was a big man.
He came to our house for four weeks.
On the fifth he went away.

SACRIFICE

One day a colonel came to tell my father
the general wanted to marry me.
Father said I was engaged.
My little sister ran around the table calling,
"Sister General. Sister General."
The colonel said father was needed to translate
a certain military document.
Nobody else could do it.
His Chinese was so excellent.

We were frightened when he did not return
after three days, four days, five days.
We had nowhere to turn.
There were no French, no Province Chief, no government.
They said they would release him
if I would marry the general.

Our house was like a funeral house.
My brother wanted to hide me.
Should we run away?
Where would we go?
My eyes were swollen with crying.

Finally, like our national heroine, Kim Van Kieu,
I realized I had no choice.
I had to pay my debt to my parents
for what they had done for me.
I would sacrifice my happiness
to save my father. I said yes.
My family demanded a large dowry
hoping the general would change his mind.

My father begged for time, saying,
"I am a big man.
I cannot marry my daughter in such haste.
I will lose face."
The general answered,
"You have three days to prepare the wedding.
I must return with my troops to China
to fight the communists."

THE WEDDING

It is the custom in an important family
for the bride to have as many clothes as possible.
Father asked for 30 ao dais,
all velvets and satins,
hoping they could not be made.
Chinese soldiers went with pistols
into the homes of the seamstresses
forcing them to sew the dresses.
They were ready by evening.

My mother's friend chose a necklace
and a diamond ring of many carats.
The whole town was forced to come to the wedding
whether they wanted to or not.
The city museum was the only place large enough.
The general ordered his troops to move everything out—
king's clothes, hats, antiques
great Cham heads and statues.

They took chairs and tables from everyone's house.
I did what I was told blindly.
The dresses were ready
jewels were brought
place was decorated
our friends were invited.
I was sent to the hairdresser.

I could not say one word to the general.
I cried silently.
My brothers refused to go to the wedding
said I was too young and innocent.
The Chinese cooks from the barracks prepared the feast.
In a dream I dressed in my red velvet dress

the white Western veil over my eyes.
There was an orchestra and the governor's piano
but no one dared to dance
with the Chinese troops all around the room.

WEDDING NIGHT

After the wedding I did not want to be alone.
I begged my father, my sisters, my mother to stay.
I pleaded with my little sister to sleep with me
all night at the barracks.
She said she would, but my mother pulled her away.
I was alone with the general.
I cried silently.

In front of me lay my guitar,
my music books, my jewels,
my new clothes—all piled up.
I told the two interpreters I would not sleep.
The general said, "Do not worry.
No one will disturb you."
After midnight he dismissed them.
I cried out loud then.
I refused to go to his bed.
All night we stayed awake at either end of a table.

It is our custom to return to our parents
the day after the wedding
to say thanks to them.
Mother looked at me.
"Are you happy?" she asked.
"Happy?" I thought.
My little sister, knowing nothing,
asked me what I did at night.
I told her I slept at the table.
She cried out, "Why did you sleep at the table
when you could have come home and slept with me?"

HONEYMOON

Each night I brought my guitar to bed
to divide me from the general.
If I felt something at night,
I would scream.
He said, "Please, please. I will do nothing.
Do not scream. The soldiers outside will laugh."

I thought of Bao.
I had seen his face at the wedding,
but said nothing
surrounded by troops and guests.

On our honeymoon at the beach in Haiphong,
the general asked my parents if I loved somebody else.
They did not know about Bao.
I told only my sister about him,
asked her to please tell him my situation
that I did not love the general.

My parents said I was the general's wife now
that the guitar between us
would not stop him
if he wanted to love me
that he must love me
not everything could be said through the interpreter.

He was tall. I was short.
He was 32. I was 18.
The moment we stepped outside the door,
we were saluted.

POOR MATCHMAKING—
A FOLK POEM

I'm climbing a ladder with a stick to catch you,
old Man in the Moon, and give you ten whacks.
After the beating I'll lash you to a tree
and give you the third degree:
Is this what you call a red thread?
Here's for your threads linking East and North!
Here's more for the ones binding husbands and wives!
Do I deserve an old hag, you matchmaking moron?
I'm climbing a ladder with a torch to burn down your house,
old bungler, old Man in the Moon.

TO CHINA

The commander general ordered my husband back to China
to Hoang Thu Phu, Kunming, not far from where I was born.
When we dropped down safely,
I did not even know the name of the airport.
The general told me not to say a word to anyone.
He did not want them to know I was Vietnamese.
He left me at a hotel.
I could not express hunger
or the need for a bath.
I learned to use signs.

Everyone was Chinese with long hair in pigtails.
It was January—cold and gloomy.
I could hear something in my ears,
but I could say nothing.
People kept toasting us as is the custom.
I could not drink
and always the same little glass was there,
the people standing and smiling.

After four weeks at the hotel
three horse-drawn buggies came to the door.
Was I going home?
The horses didn't answer.
They hung their heads as we loaded the carriages.
We drove out to the countryside.
Where we stopped, thirty people
came out to greet us.

I saw an ancestor's altar.
Nearby was a lady staring at me,
not too old and not too young.
She was as small as I

with a round face, small eyes
and a big mouth covered in red lipstick.
She wore a blue Chinese dress.
Was it his sister?

Then I knew. It was the other wife.
The general made a motion I did not understand—
to pay respects to the other wife,
the little wife to the bigger one.
He looked at me, motioning to nod my head.
Then his whole family came out,
his three children,
and the old men with beards.
They all knelt on the floor to me.

OUR MARRIED LIFE

The house was surrounded by rice fields.
A mountain stood in the distance.
In the front courtyard was a well
and a flower garden with orange trees.
A mirror hung on the front door
to ward away spirits.
An inner door protected the house from evil
as evil follows a straight line.
Yet, only a fortuneteller knew
from which direction evil would come.

I lived on the first floor,
the first wife on the second floor.
Whenever the general came to my room,
she would throw things, make a scene.
Once she tried to poison me.
The general, suspecting her,
gave my rice to the dog
who vomited and died.

He moved me to a different house
where Mai and Vinh were born.
He was fighting then in the West
against Mao's troops.
I stayed at home with the children
and two soldiers he left with me.

I knew the Chinese characters
and at last could speak and write.
I kept my pencil and ink in the study room.
Thin paper was specially divided for each character.
When he was home on leave,

the general taught me handwriting
said I had an inborn sense of it.

His sister, my friend, helped me,
saying, "It is not a sin to have two wives.
My brother has no sons."
When Vinh was born, we celebrated for three months
dyed the eggs red.
I began to like the general better.
He was my closest friend now
who taught me everything I knew.

SEA MOUNTAIN

In China I traveled with two soldiers
who carried me up my favorite Sea Mountain.
At the base we ate raw snails
covered with nut seasoning, chopped mint.
We climbed the path of Five Mountains
until the clouds ran between our knees
until the sound of the brass bells
echoing across the mountains
rang closer and closer.

We climbed little steps
higher and higher
until the stream shone silver
and the people below us were tiny.
At the top stood a beautiful pagoda
with five hundred gold-leaf Buddhas.
People came to the pagoda
to burn incense, to ask their fortune
gain answers from the Buddhas
from papers at the base of each statue.

I would stay there for days
in a house built in the rocks.
I fished in the small streams.
In the summer we played mah-jongg in the rock house.
We played five so one person could sleep.
All night we shuffled the ivory pieces
under the light of the kerosene lamps.

Once coming home from there,
pirates robbed my jewelry.
They took everything—

gold chains, diamond rings, jade.
When I dared to tell my mother years later,
she cried, "You have lost yours
and your children's property."

OUTSIDE MY HOUSE

Revisiting the clear pond of my childhood,
I looked down from above
on the two stone dragons.
From the mouth of one came green water,
from the other black.

As a child
I wanted to hold the cold water in my hand.
My mother stopped me,
whispering, "The dragons are sacred.
You must not touch them."

I remember in mountain lakes
the protected fish
black, pink, silver—
their mouths breaking the surface
of the still water
to eat the popped corn we threw.

The pond and lakes seemed small when I grew up,
but I still loved the spring peach blossoms
green willows in my courtyard
the warm summer rain
giant chrysanthemums in autumn.

I was happy outside my house.

BURNING OUR HOUSE
IN HADONG

I received a letter from my mother saying
my second brother had burnt down our beloved house.
The Viet Minh, in their fight against the French,
ordered my family to destroy our dwelling.
My brother poured gasoline over the walls of the house
then set a torch to it.

As the flames leaped up,
he remembered the piano
so he tried to pull it through the door.
When he realized he could not save the piano,
he began beating it with a hammer—
all the time laughing and crying.

My family was forced to run from the house
by Allied bombing against the Viet Minh.
They heard the alert and ran, sometimes for miles
through the rice fields and jungle around Hadong.
When they saw the planes overhead,
they would lie down in the ditches
at the borders of the rice fields,
pretending to be dead.

The planes would dive out of the sky
and fire along the ground.
My father threw away the rice
when it got too heavy.
My mother threw away her sandals
when they broke on the rocky paths.
They cooked very little
for fear the planes would see the smoke
from their small fires.

They stayed where they could
in a rice field, in a village hut.
The people knew of my father and welcomed him.
When the place was unsafe, they ran again—
from the bombing, from the French, from the Viet Minh,
it did not matter, they had to run.
Sometimes their new hosts ran with them.
For one year they lived this way.

My family and others like them
were caught in the middle:
afraid the French would think them Viet Minh
and kill them,
afraid the Viet Minh would think them French agents
and kill them.

Far away in China, I held onto my new baby daughter
and prayed for my family.

RETURN TO HANOI

When the general was surrounded
at Tien Sy in the mountains,
he sent his captain galloping back
with word for me to leave China.
I took my two children and my guitar
and flew home to Hanoi.

My mother and my elder sister were at the airport.
My sister said, "This is my baby and this is my husband."
I saw Bao standing beside her
and then could see nothing else
only people calling my name in the distance.
I said I was airsick from the long trip.

I tried to avoid him
not wishing any complications,
but he wrote me every day
saying he never expected to see me again.
He said he had told my sister he still loved me
and that we should marry.
I said, "I have a husband.
Let bygones be bygones."

I was back in Hanoi only one month
when I received word my husband had been killed.
The whole family cried,
but tears did not come to my eyes.
They could not.
Bao kept writing for months and months.
I kept refusing
afraid my sister might kill herself.
She had slashed her wrist once before.

MARRIAGE TO BAO

Bao still wanted to marry me
after three years of formal mourning for the general.
He said many people in his family had two wives
including his father.
He was the son of the second wife.
My father said he had not known
of my love for Bao,
but now that he did, we should marry.
He said it was normal in our country
for two sisters to have one husband.
Bao's mother agreed.
I said yes reluctantly,
not wanting anyone outside the family to know.
We were married and had two children.
After the second, we became like brother and sister.
I could not stand my sister's long face,
her jealousies, her unhappiness.
Blood runs thick in my country.

Bao decided that since I was more educated,
I would be the outside wife,
my sister the inside wife.
I would entertain his friends and business associates.
She would take care of his house.
We lived this way in different houses for six years.
I was eager to work, but was forbidden by Father and Bao.
My father tore up my acceptance
from the Ministry of Education.
I had to teach music at home.

SAIGON
SWANSEA
RANGOON
SAIGON
1954-1975

GENEVA AGREEMENTS

We were told in 1954
that anyone not wishing
to live with the communists
could go south by plane or by boat.

My father wanted to leave,
said he knew the communists.
My mother had spent much of her life
in the four walls of our houses.
She did not want to go
to a strange new place.

My younger sister's husband
had been in Saigon.
He warned us against
the unfriendly people there
said he would never go back.

We were given 300 days to decide.

SEEING MY
THIRD BROTHER, BANG

We received word that my third brother
whom we had not heard from in many years
wanted to see us.
He said he could not come to our house
so Father and I rented a rickshaw.
We left early in the morning
reaching his village in the afternoon.

A bamboo hedge surrounded the village.
We have an ancient saying,
"The power of the Emperor stops at the bamboo hedge."
We walked through a bamboo gate
down a dirt path until we reached a thatched house.

Two men came toward us.
One held back a barking dog.
The other led us to my brother.
He looked so thin and different
as he bowed to my father.
I stood behind my father.
We all cried.

When Father was asleep,
my brother asked me to come into the yard.
We remembered our childhood together.
We called him *mot sach,* the bookworm.
He said the Viet Minh were good people
who believed in giving to the poor
saving the country for the Vietnamese.

I said I had no contact with them,
but that Father said they were against families.

My brother said the nationalists were sentimentalists,
just like we were, with a strong sense of family.
He promised if I stayed he'd help me build a new life,
take care of the children.

We talked through the night
and I decided to stay in the North,
I remember sitting in the moonlight
watching the chickens go back and forth in the yard.
He drew me a map of our rendezvous spot
told me not to bring much luggage.
I would not need many things.

I WAS CAUGHT

The night of the 18th July
all the family was packed
to go to Gia Lam airport.
I could not sleep.
I had packed my bags
and put them a little to one side.
My mother sensed my plan.
She came over to my bed and asked,
"You are not coming with us?"

She cried out, waking everyone
and brought my father to my bed, saying,
"Here is your daughter
who will not come with us."
He asked if I planned to stay behind
with my third brother.
I tried to say no, but the tears came.

Father said we must stick together
at least share our troubles.
The communists would divide the family.
This way we would die together.
The whole family slept near me that night.
In the morning, they put me in the car first
with the little children.
I could not get a message to my brother.

WHAT WE LEFT,
WHAT WE TOOK

We were leaving Hanoi by American military planes.
We were each allowed forty pounds.
We took no furniture, only gold.
Father took his scroll with the nine birds.
His second wife went separately.
Unknown to us, he had married
the woman we had chased down Kham Thien Street.

Bao's sister had no children.
She loved babies.
She was my friend, loved me more than my sister.
I told her I was going South
and planned to work, against everyone's wishes.
I feared I could not do it all
with a small child.
At the last minute, I left Bao's little girl with her.

SAIGON MARKET

I was scared to go out at first,
even to the market.
We spent the day looking from the window
at people going back and forth.
There were huge Cambodian women
who talked very loud
staring at you from head to toe
as if they would swallow you up.
They spoke Vietnamese,
but we could not understand them.
Their minds had been poisoned against us.
"Why do you come here?" they asked.
"It is too crowded already.
You just want to follow the westerners
for their bread and butter."
They recognized us by our voices,
our clothes, our skin.
When they saw us, they raised their prices
and we did not dare bargain.

One day at the market,
my long ao dai knocked over a woman's lichee basket.
She scolded me until a mob came
and started ripping my dress
calling out, "Hurt that northerner.
They have come to make us suffer."
A policeman came.
When they saw he too was from the North,
they yelled, "Kill him. Kill them both."
Finally a third came, from the South.
He tried to calm the mob, saying,
"This lady is your countrywoman.

She has left everything behind.
She suffers too. Please."

It was a long time before I went back
to the market. When I did,
I always took a southerner with me.
I carried my plastic bag in silence.

OUR HOUSE IN CHOLON

It was hard to find a house in Saigon.
One million people had moved south.
At first we stayed in part of a friend's house
across from the old cinema.
Father said we could not stay there forever.
Every day we went searching for a house.
We finally found one in Cholon,
the Chinese city within Saigon.
We could speak to few of the Chinese there.
They spoke Cantonese, not Mandarin.

We all contributed our gold, our jewelry.
Nine of us squeezed into the tiny place—
only two rooms and a kitchen.
The dining room became wall-to-wall cots.
At night the baby would wake everyone.
To get up we would crawl from one cot to another.
Outside, was a public outhouse,
really a big dirty can.
You had to wait in line.
I was so shy I would get up at five.

Soon we looked for a new house.
I found one on Nancy Street.
The French had used it for a school.
There were 36 houses in a row—all in ruins,
36 families worked to clean them up.
The market was in the front,
gambling in the back.
This was the house my father liked.
He was 63 when we moved to Saigon.
He died there at 84.

SOUTHERNERS AND
NORTHERNERS

The South has only two seasons
dry and rainy.
In the North we had four.
In the South they eat sweeter food
with more coconut sauce.
In the North farmers rise at 3
to go to the rice paddies
no matter how cold it is.

Northerners work harder.
They plan for the future.
If I make 1000 piasters, I save 300
one day to buy a tael of gold.
In the South they spend it all.
They do not take life as seriously,
do not have death on their minds.
Even the farmers move easily
through their sunny fields.

A POEM ABOUT THE NORTH

(memorized from a schoolbook when I was 8)

December is the month we grow potatoes.
January we grow beans.
February we grow eggplant.
March we harrow the fields.
April we prepare the rice seedlings.
Everyone works.
The husband harrows.
The wife plants.
We are happy.
In May we finish harvesting.
Thanks to heaven each hectare yields
5 full buckets of rice.
I must grind and beat the full bucket.
The husk we use for cooking.
We beat it again, removing the second layer
producing the very white rice.
The hull we feed to the pigs
mixed with water lilies from the ponds.
I must pay the tax from the harvest
for my husband.
If we be hungry or full
we must be together always.
Better to be poor and together than alone.

GOING TO WORK

I went to work in the Ministry of Social Welfare.
My mother was furious.
Being old-fashioned, she thought other people
would think she and my father
did not have enough to feed me.
They would lose face.

I trained as a midwife and social assistant
helping poor families in hospitals
and in their homes where they suffered family breakdowns.
I helped some of the million people from the North
find their lost relatives.

Mother scolded me for leaving my house and children.
I explained I needed something for myself,
needed to have a job and responsibility,
money to provide for my children.
She refused to talk to me.
Ridiculed at home, I advanced at work
from door-to-door fieldwork
to planning in the hospitals.

FIGHTING

I cannot forget one night in March of 1955.
It was midnight.
The whole family was asleep.
We heard guns,
the sound of people running toward the Y Bridge.
We all woke up and looked out the window.
We saw soldiers running.
At first we thought it was the military.
We saw different uniforms.
Then we thought it was the communists.
We all hid under our thick dining-room table.
We covered the top of the table
with our pillows and blankets.
The fighting went on around us until morning.
Then the shots got less and less
and we dared to open the door.
The neighbors said one side was the military police,
the other the Binh Xuyen, Vietnamese against the government.
At 2 o'clock I decided I must go to work
or the government would question me.
Tanks were lined up near the bus.
Suddenly the fighting started again.
There were people all around me
and I was caught in the middle
unable to get back to my house.
A soldier behind me
dropped to the ground covered with blood.
I started running,
not knowing in which direction.

RUNNING TO ESCAPE

I came to a flooded place,
the houses all on stilts.
We call them *pierres sur pilotes*.
I climbed up into the houses.
Then I saw the fire at my back.
Trying to jump over the water,
I landed in it, waves slapping all around me.
I ripped my green-and-white ao dai,
lost my new sandals
but managed to run, wet and barefoot over small stones.
I heard people shouting, but I did not see them.
I crawled into a bunker
covered with wide planks.
It was dark in there, but I heard a noise.
I turned and there was a yellow dog
as scared as I was.
He put his paw in my hand
to show that he needed me.
We both knelt in the dark hole, listening.
I heard a wind whirling over us.
I poked my head out
to see all the roofs on fire.
I knew I would have to run from my safe place.
The dog ran out with me.
The two of us, running, running.
He barking, me too scared to cry.
After hours I saw the Saigon market
and knew I had run in a circle.
The fire was chasing me
smoke billowing all around
until I fell down unconscious.
The shots seemed further away.
It was cooler.

WAR IN THE STREETS

When I woke up,
I saw a man on a bicycle.
I stopped him, begged him to help me.
"Please. I cannot run or walk."
He asked if I knew how to ride a bike.
I said no but I could sit behind him.
He said he could not ride toward the fire.
It would be suicide.
On the way to his sister's, I recognized a road
and got off, thanking the man.

My mother's friend cried when she saw me
walking alone toward her house.
"Where is your family?
Where are your children?
You live where the fire comes from."
I stayed the night, returning home the next day.
I said I would rather die with my family.
I walked home slowly in sandals borrowed from their daughter.

The police tried to stop me from going near my house,
but I begged them to let me see my family.
Then I saw all of them alive—standing outside the door.
They were so happy to see me. Mother thought I was dead.
They had been trapped by the fire,
but our house was saved by the wind turning suddenly.
The ones at the back were burnt to the ground.
The wall of our house was full of bullet holes.

We believe in destiny.
Mother said she had prayed to Buddha.
For many generations our family had done nothing wrong
so this time Buddha protected us.

LOOKING FOR VOTES

We always thought we would go home to Hanoi.
Two years in the South, then with America's help
we would defeat the communists.
With America on our side, how could we lose?

In 1955 Diem proclaimed us a republic.
We were sent in groups from the ministries
to the villages to influence people
to vote for Diem as president.

We would bring food, explain his aims,
said we would vote for him.
At first I was afraid to speak.
They would know I was from the North.
They'd accuse me of taking a good government job.

The women in the South smoke and drink
and are generally easygoing.
We could hardly keep from laughing
when they offered us their cheap cigars.

They called their children
by where they came in the family
number two, three, four, five:
cau hai, cau ba, cau tu, cau nam

but never number one.
Number one son was called number two.
The name *number one* was reserved
for the head of the village, *ong ca*, Mr. One.

I would walk through the rice fields,
ask to enter their wooden houses,
sit with them as their children crawled
across the floor with the pigs and the chickens.

HOMESICK

In the South, I lost my interest in playing music.
The family was split up.
The heat burnt.
The streets were filled with noise and fighting.

At night I would stare from my bed
through the window
at the moonlight shining on the leaves.

I felt lonely.
Parts of Hoang Duong's song of the North
drifted over me with the breezes.

"Hanoi, oh my darling,
from an immeasurable distance I think of you
a city decorated with brilliant lights
and the colored, floating flaps of the ao dai.

"Hanoi, oh my darling,
in the endless raining evenings,
remember there is someone alone
in silence watching the floating clouds
my heart broken from missing you."

I thought of the house of my childhood.
Clear nights singing with my brothers and sisters
in the courtyard by the imitation mountain.

LEARNING ENGLISH

I decided to learn English.
Bao taught me one hour a day.
He learned from the radio.
My parents did not understand.
"What are you learning that for?"
they would ask in scorn.
"The sound is so strange to us.
Your place is in the home.
You should not be seen with foreigners."

When Bao was given a scholarship
to study administration in the States,
I encouraged him to go.
He wrote me saying,
"The longer I am in the States,
the more I realize how poor our country is.
There is no civil war here.
If you have a will, you can succeed.
Women have more freedom
and divorce is easier."

THE AMERICAN CAPTAIN

In Washington Bao met an American colonel
on his way to do duty in Saigon.
He wanted to know Vietnamese people
and became a friend to me.
His wife taught me English.
I would help them buy Vietnamese things,
ceramics, elephants, tortoise-shell, lacquer work.
I also attended English classes
at the Vietnamese-American Association.
Our teachers were officers
who came from the camps to teach us.
My teacher was a black captain.
He was a doctor.
He looked at me all the time in class.
My friends said he was in love with me.
He began to walk with me,
to follow me to the bus station.
I did not know what to do—
a foreigner and black.
I was scared of him,
only bar-girls walked with foreigners.
I convinced my friend Mr. Tuan
from the Finance Ministry to walk home with me.

LOSING FACE

One day after the captain had been absent,
he asked in front of the whole class,
"Nga, you have not even asked me what happened.
Every night when I close my eyes, I see your image."
I wanted to disappear.
My face was red; my fingers numb.
I stood up, took my books and left.
Angry and sick for the whole week,
I could not go to class.
One day I saw him pass by my house.
I wanted to hide.
He had something under his arm,
candy for the children, perfume, soap,
everything from the PX.
The family and neighbors were shocked.
No foreigners had been to our neighborhood.
They all came out to watch.
We were surrounded by people.
I said, "This is my English teacher.
He has come to visit me, to see my children."
He asked me where I had been
said I must return to class
that he had done nothing wrong
except love me.

I had nowhere to turn.
I asked the American colonel for help.
He asked for the captain's name and serial number
and had him transferred.
I did not go back to the training classes.

MY CAREER

I wanted to leave my country
to train in another, hopefully in the States.
I passed six different tests
but my Big Boss refused to recommend me.
I think he kept my tests in his desk drawer.
I became so enraged that I finally asked him
why he did not send me.
This was considered very blunt in my country.
(I did not know then that he was anti-American
the leader of a Buddhist league.)

He said I must stay in my country
go to the provinces and help our poor.
Once I had proven myself, I could go abroad.
I was so furious, I volunteered for Chuong Thien,
one of the most dangerous provinces.
It was a poor area, attacked daily by the communists.
The roads were mined.
I arranged through USAID
to fly back and forth by plane.

The Chief of the Province had a bomb shelter under his house.
He too preferred to spend his nights in Saigon.
He was a good military officer, but spoke no English.
I became his interpreter to the Americans.
To build his own reputation,
he asked for material goods,
food, blankets and building materials.

Trained in the social services,
I knew we needed a headquarters
to receive people, to meet them.
Within three months, I set up a day-care center

and a sewing class
much to the surprise of the Big Boss
who had to sign the papers
for my scholarship to England.

ENGLAND

I studied in Swansea in South Wales.
England was freezing even in July.
They took us to a shopping center to buy new coats.
The streets were dark and gloomy—
all stone and centuries old.
I felt lonely, quiet and strange.

My Vietnamese friend and I stayed in the attic
of a professor's house.
The flower pot on the table froze.
We used all our money in electric heaters.
We put pennies in the machines,
burned our money all winter.

Studying juveniles, neglected children,
I spent many hours with my face in a dictionary.
The library was a huge place
with 36,000 books.

At night I would cover my feet
with a hot-water bottle.
Listening to the English wind
howl under my door,
I'd think of the soft air in my country,
the songs of our village.

MY HOME VILLAGE—
A SONG

Golden sunshine glitters through the trees
in the late afternoon.

Birds sing their jovial songs.

Leaning on doors, villagers stand and sit
sharing memories of their lives.

Across the sky wind hums through bamboo flutes
attached to paper kites.

The golden rice dances as if joining in the gaiety.

O afternoon in my country, how tranquil and peaceful you are.

I wait in the silence, watching the blue smoke rise,
waiting to fall in love.

BURMA

Before I reached home, I visited Rangoon as a tourist.
When I arrived at the Vietnamese consulate, Bao was there.
Without my knowing, he had transferred
to the Ministry of Foreign Affairs,
Vice-Consul to Burma.

In Saigon he had seen my application for another scholarship
to allow me to stay out of the country longer.
He had put it away in a drawer.
I was surprised and furious.
I was happier alone.

My son had been expelled from school.
He was intelligent and trusted no one,
not the government, not the school, not me.
He did not want to serve in the army.
When I said, "How can we beat the communists
if you do not fight?"

He answered
"Whom will I fight—my uncle?
Big shots do not have to fight.
Why should I?
You will not have to go to the battlefield.
You know nothing."
My father blamed me for his attitudes,
said I neglected him when I went to work.

All my plans for my own career were ruined.
Bao organized a big party
introduced me as his wife
told me diplomatic wives cannot work
and sent for his mother and the older children.
My sister stayed with the younger children in Saigon.

CORRUPTION

In Rangoon we stayed in the same house
as the Consul General.
We had a cook, a gardener and a driver.
The house had two stories
and a garden where I spent most of my time.
There were snakes and scorpions
that lay on the rocks in the sun.
The Burmese, Buddhists, do not believe in killing snakes.

My job was to entertain guests.
The consul would say we had 150 guests, instead of 50.
He rented the house with dollars from the Saigon government.
He changed the money on the black market
and kept the difference.
He claimed false renovations on the villa.
By these corrupt means, he made thousands.

He offered my husband money
asked him to falsify a document.
When Bao refused, the Consul made a report back to Saigon
that I was a mistress.
We have a saying:

> *"Once you fight with a snake,*
> *you must smash his head.*
> *Otherwise, he will kill you."*

Without the Consul's permission
Bao returned to Saigon to plead his case.
When he arrived, his name was already smeared.
They said he was a playboy
flitting from one woman to another.

The Consul had stolen so much money,
he could "please" the commission.

We have another saying,
"A dog always finds his way home."

TET
JANUARY 31, 1968

We had to come back to Saigon for Tet.
Everyone was meeting at my mother's and father's.
I could see my children.
My daughter was in boarding school in Dalat.
My son would be home from the Air Force.

Tet, New Year's, is our celebration day.
The whole family gathers
dressed in their best clothes
to give thanks to Heaven
and to our ancestors.
We have a saying:
> *Birds have nests.*
> *People have ancestors.*

Everything must be ready
before the end of the lunar year.
Our tradition says
we must be quiet on that night
at peace to receive the new spring.

We prepare special food.
In the North, we have sweet oranges,
in the South, mangosteens, watermelon, tangerines.
We invite our ancestors to eat
offering them the feast at an altar
the best place in the house.

We light incense on the altar.
When the sticks burn to the end,
we light others.

When they have burned,
our ancestors have finished.
We remove the food and serve ourselves.

On the fifth day
we prepare another big feast.
We burn red tissue paper
covered with gold and silver paint—
false money for our ancestors
to spend on transportation to their world.

To prepare for Tet,
we made sticky rice together.
This takes 24 hours
and must cook at the same temperature.
We put logs around a huge pot
which holds 50 rice cakes.
Someone must watch the pot all night
to keep the rice from drying out.

Early in the morning
during my turn to watch the rice cakes,
I heard shots far away.
The next day there was fighting
on the Y Bridge again
people crying and running,
uniforms everywhere.

We learned through a radio
this was a surprise attack by the Viet Cong.
They attacked the American embassy,
American bases, every town and city in South Vietnam.
Many of them came into Saigon in trucks

hidden under Tet watermelons.
Like my son, many South Vietnamese soldiers
were home for the New Year.

We stayed together in our concrete house,
not daring to look out the window.

CORRUPTION

After the Tet Offensive,
the corruption grew worse and worse.
What we had seen in Burma
was a mirror of life in Saigon.
Always the Americans worked hand-in-glove
with the Vietnamese.

All the buses leaving Long Binh Base
had false hollows under the seats
filled with steaks, chickens, bacon.
As soon as the buses were out the gate,
everything was sold.
There was no bargaining then.

I had a woman friend
who bought a truck for 2 million piasters.
People inside the American warehouse
would load the truck with goods.
No guard would inspect it.
Everyone was in on the deal.

They drove to the jungle, distributed the goods.
Once they loaded hundreds of boxes
thinking they were radios.
When they opened the boxes and found computers
that no one could understand,
they threw them in the river.

THE SYSTEM

The Americans were too rich.
They thought they could buy everything.
They were poor psychologists.
They gave lots of money to the man on top
and did not watch down the line.
On paper, the projects looked good,
but the money went out the door.

The Project Chief drew up a plan
for a Community Center.
He said he needed so many sewing machines,
so many blankets.
In the meeting with the American advisor,
the translator would say
we need fifty sewing machines.

The place was built.
There was a big celebration.
Everyone came and lots of pictures were taken.
Ten sewing machines were in the showroom,
the other forty had been sold.
Who was there to check?

It was simple.
If you were corrupt, you stayed on top,
had money for your family.
If you worked under these corrupt officials
and were not,
you were sent to the battlefields.

If you had money, you were not sent.
If you failed a course at the university,
you could buy a pass and avoid the army.

I knew someone who flunked
and ended up teaching French to a general's children.

If you deserted and the MPs found you hiding,
you bribed the MPs.
If you went to the doctor, you paid him
to falsify your check-up.
You drank something that showed up
on the X-ray of your lung.

We have a saying:
*"Money can go through paper
no matter how thick."*

TWO DEATHS

When my father's second wife died,
he begged us to come to the funeral,
said she had never done us any harm.
My mother was stone-faced, but we went.

Soon after the funeral, father had a stroke.
Suddenly when he was gambling,
his hands went down.
He could not answer my mother.

I rushed home to give him massage,
but he could not speak.
He came to stay with me for three years.
We cared for him, washed him every day.

He showed great courage, regained his speech
and even helped my daughter with her French,
but he remained paralyzed and could not travel.
He died six months before we left the country.

Otherwise, we might still be there.

MY FATHER'S FUNERAL

We believe the devil may come
to lead the soul of the dead to Hell
before the burial.

We wrapped my father's body
in Buddha's orange robe
so Buddha would lead his soul to Heaven.

A monk circled the coffin.
The family, dressed in white gauze mourning clothes
and white turbans, chanted prayers.

The eldest son walked in front of the coffin
carrying an incense burner.

The grandchildren wore white headbands.
The great-grandchildren wore yellow.
The great-great-grandchildren red.

Old friends brought flowers and banners—
more than 100 of them—
with words for the dead.

The coffin was closed and nailed shut.
The family walked behind it to the grave.

We believe the dead must be buried deep and tight
so the soul will be secure and go to Heaven
and bless the family.

If not, the soul will become a monster
and haunt the family.

We believe members of the family
with the same sign
must stay away at the closing of the coffin.

My father was the sign of the buffalo.
One of my brothers was also.
We fear the dead wants one of his own for company.

100 DAYS

For 100 days after my father died,
we prepared his favorite dishes
worshiped at his house altar
with the huge incense burner
the white candles
his picture wrapped in black satin.

We believe after the body is buried properly,
the soul floats with nowhere to go for 49 days.
It must be fed so as not to do mischief.

For the next 51 days, the soul goes to the intermediate state
where the good deeds are weighed against the bad.
If bad, it will be reincarnated as an animal,

if good, as a human again.
If best, it will go to Paradise
never to be reborn again.

MY SIXTH BROTHER, TUOC, RETURNS TO HANOI

During the Paris Accords,
my seventh brother was assigned by the government
to go to Hanoi on an observation trip
to check on the North's claims about prisoner exchange.

He was chaperoned by communists
but managed to pass by our last house
hoping to see our brothers and sister.

The house was the same pale color.
All the windows were closed.
Tall weeds grew on the path.
He felt no life there
only silence and gloom.

He wished there had been a bird.
He would tie a note to its leg
to carry up to the window.

The note would say:

"Here I am. I have come back
to visit my sister and my brother
and my country. Where are they?"

THE MAGAZINE

When the American magazine came to me,
I was ready to leave my job.
I'd hoped to do family planning,
new foster homes for children.
I'd seen them work in other countries.

I knew the fraud in mine.
The women in Saigon who moved the same 200 children
from orphanage to orphanage
receiving money from the state each time.

My boss laughed at my ideas
said I lived in a dream world.
Our country was at war.
I should put my ideas away for a decade.
He used me as an interpreter
to talk to the Americans.

In my country, one cannot resign
from civil service during war.
It would mean jail.
I had to show I was incapable
with a report of five doctors
who said I had a mental disturbance.

Then I resigned.
The magazine hired me to watch over the books,
make sure nobody was stealing from the company.
They called me Madame Nga.

THE AMERICANS

The Americans came to Vietnam
and turned our country upside down
with their money and their army.

Their soldiers slept with our women.
Their generals patted our generals on the heads
as if they were children.

Bao and I had a successful business at first
selling Vietnamese handicrafts at the PX,
silver, ceramics, lacquerware.

Inflation rose higher and higher.
I thought we should get out.
Bao said no.

"America is so strong,
the richest, most powerful country in the world.

Number one in the world. She will never desert us.
She cannot. She is in too deep.

She will send more ammunition.
NBC and CBS say so.

She will bring more phantoms and battleships
and B-52s to bomb Hanoi."

THE NOODLE CART

My boss's wife was educated.
She taught English literature at the university.
She called the office and asked questions,
"Why is Chi Phuc crying?
Why don't Vietnamese eat cheese?"
One day she asked me to find a noodle cart
to take home to the United States.
She was my boss's wife. Of course I would do it.

It took me three weeks of searching.
I would go from cart to cart
asking where to buy one.
No one would tell me.
I got Bao to drive me through Cholon
way out to the countryside to PhuLam
where I had never been.

Every week I went to the same noodle man
pretending I went for noodles.
Soon he knew what I liked
and we started talking.
He asked if I wanted to start a business.
I explained my boss's wife
wanted the cart as a souvenir.
He said the Chinese would never sell
except to another Chinese.
After 14 bowls, he told me where to go look.

Bao said I was spending too much time on the project.
I said I had made a promise and I would keep it.
I would go by cyclo if he would not take me.
One Saturday we drove round and round for two hours
to a place where there were few houses.

Far away, all lined up in a field, we saw the noodle carts.
There were only Chinese there.
They said no carts would be ready for six months.

Finally I found a man in Saigon
who wanted to sell his cart.
He had a second wife in Can Tho
and wanted to move down with her.
The father and son fought.
The father refused to sell.
The son said he had to. The father cried.
The son told me to sneak back in the evening
and take the cart.
I had to find people to push it to the warehouse.

My boss's wife was pleased with the noodle cart.
"It's perfect," she said.
She had it shipped home to the United States.

LEAVING
SAIGON
1975

THE GAME OF CHESS

The Bureau Chiefs came and the Bureau Chiefs went.
We had to get used to them.

One played chess with my colleague.
My colleague always won.

The Big Boss's face would turn red.
Then he'd come over and kick my desk.

The Americans expressed themselves
more than the Vietnamese.

One day my colleague said, "This isn't worth it,"
and let the Big Boss win.

DECIDING

We went to the office every day.
Though the situation was critical,
people at work said nothing.
Province Chiefs were running.
We told the Big Boss our country would be lost.
We told him we would blow ourselves up
if we could not leave.

I sat at my desk doing the financial report.
My thoughts went round and round.

Should I leave?
Should I go alone?
Should I take my mother?
She did not want to go.
She feared they wouldn't let her chew the betel.
Should I leave my children?
How would I make a living?
What would happen when the communists came?

When I made up my mind,
pictures of my childhood floated to the surface
as clear and strong as dreams.

Our old house in Hadong.
The bamboo in the backyard.
We ate the shoots.
The soldiers made a fence from the stalks.
My sister and I painted the fence
first white, then blue, then her favorite yellow.
The small antigonon vine we planted
with its pink blossoms in spring.

Our ponds.
The many steps down
to the small bridge
where we'd sit hour after hour
letting our hands dip into the water
trying to catch the silver-brown fish.

Airplanes bombing
running from our house
people dying, people calling from outside the walls
don't take me. I'm not dead yet.
The family hiding together in our house in Cholon
sunlight coming through the bullet holes.

THE SECRET LIST

The Big Boss said a plane would come
and fly us to Hong Kong.

We were to make a list of our family.

Only the staffers and the immediate family
could be on the list.

We were to talk to no one
or the plan would fail.

THE TELEX OPERATOR

Linh, the telex operator, could not be on the list.
He was not a full-time staffer.
He worked in the evenings,
sometimes all night, sleeping on the couch
because of the time difference to the States.
He asked me what are they doing in New York
buying bread and shipping merchandise to Hong Kong?
I could not tell him
we were the bread and the merchandise.
That was the code.
Someone must have told him.
His wife came to the office crying,
"Sister, sister are you trying to run away?
Would you leave us behind?"
I knew she had ten children.
She said she would bring them all
to lie down in front of my door.

We knew that if there were too many of us,
we would all be caught.
Linh had been there eight years,
one year longer than I.
He was from the North.
I knew if he were left behind,
he would throw a grenade
and blow his whole family up.
I brought his case to the Big Boss.
When the confidential came over the wire
from New York saying he could go,
we all cried. He was overhappy,
said I had saved his whole family.
After that, all plans were kept secret from me.

FIRST, WE MUST TAKE
OURSELVES

At the end I was so scared,
I did not feel like myself.
I did not know what to take,
what to leave behind.
I told the children,
"First, we must take ourselves."

We were silent for two-and-a-half months.
No one talked.
My sister had swollen eyes.
We had no appetite.
I made my son a waistband
to carry our gold.

The manager of the Continental Hotel
stopped me and asked,
"You look sad. Are you all right?
Are you planning to go away?"
"No," I said. "Are you?"
He said no. "I am old.
It will not be too bad."

PHOTOGRAPHS

We could bring only
what fit into one small bag.
They warned us not to take too much.
"They have things in the States,"
the Big Boss said.

For days I burnt documents on my terrace,
papers from when I worked for my government
papers from when I worked for the Americans.
I couldn't think
except to destroy whatever would bring trouble.

I burnt photographs
of the whole family at Tet,
year after year
all of us together
my father's nine birds.

I stared at the black-and-white pictures:
me—tiny, smiling
a pigtail on both sides
holding my eldest brother's hand,

me—the angel in the school play
a tiara on my head,
me in China at the bottom of Sea Mountain
my children standing beside me.

As the pile of ashes floated away
I felt I was burning my life.

PACKING

I packed strange things
sandalwood soap from Hong Kong,
12 of my best ao dai,
my collection of tiny perfume bottles.

We all wanted to bring our mothers.
None of us could.
We had so many false starts
I never said goodbye to her.

One morning I made an incense offering
on my father's altar.

"You going today?" Mother asked.
"No," I said. "I just missed him
dreamt about him
wanted him to wish us luck."

I left my mother in our house on the street
that had been named General de Gaulle,
then Cong Ly, or Justice Street,
and then Cach Mang, Revolution Street.

I left my money on the outside porch
and never saw her again.

PAPER MONEY

One of Bao's daughters saved a million piasters.
She kept it too long.

On the last day
she carried the money in a bag
running through the streets of Saigon
trying to exchange it for anything.

The boy at the Continental Hotel
gave her $2.00 for it.

If he hadn't,
she would have thrown the bag away
money and all.
It was too heavy to carry.

OUTSIDE THE GATES

In the end, we had falsified documents.
I had to pretend I was the wife
of one of the American correspondents,
who came to plan our escape.
On the appointed day, we were the lead car,
four others followed.
When the correspondent asked if I minded saying
I was his wife, I just laughed.
We went through the security gate without stopping.
The guards whistled,
put their guns at the ready.
I said, "Please stop."
They ordered us from the cars.
I said I had come to see my husband off.
They said I could go, not my children.
They had new orders,
no Vietnamese allowed at the airport.
Had they seen our sons' real papers,
they would have been jailed.
They were supposed to be in the army.
We tried all the gates.
The Big Boss put 500,000 piasters
in with our papers.
The money was returned.
The guard said, "A few days ago
these papers would have been legal. Not now."
We tried dollars.
Nothing worked.
Five hours and we were still outside the gates.

INTO THE AIRPORT

There were 23 in our group,
all from foreign news agencies.
Bao and my sister went separately.
By late afternoon our chartered plane had departed
with us still outside the gates.

We regrouped and returned
this time in an embassy car
its windows covered on all sides by curtains.
No one could see in.
We were stopped by a Vietnamese MP
before reaching the hangar,
but he was told by an American
to let us pass.
We were in!

All the planes had gone.
The Big Boss told us to stay,
made me responsible for the group,
said he would look for us in Guam,
gave us 20,000 piasters for dinner,
wished us luck and left.

THE AIRPORT

In the yard outside the hangar
were hundreds of Vietnamese
lying on their mats with their luggage
and their children all around them.
We were worried about the crowds,
about being searched,
about the gold and dollars on our persons,
about what we would say if we were caught.
We walked to the snack bar for dinner
and paid 19,000 piasters for noodles.
When we got back, it was dark.
Our spot was crowded with people,
embassy people, MACV people.
My son thought he recognized a secret agent
and hid his face.
Men with walkie-talkies were everywhere.

When an official Vietnamese asked us
to leave our place,
I pleaded with an American Lt.-Colonel
who allowed us to stay.
We had a tiny baby with us, my granddaughter.
I told him we had missed our charter
and wanted to go as soon as possible.
He said the sooner the better.
I said the office could not blame us
if we did not take the plane they had chartered.
He said to stay together
and go to the Philippines, not to Guam.
I said, anywhere but Vietnam.

ESCAPE

We made lists.
That was the manifest,
name, sex, age.
When the captain came for us,
we went quickly to the bus,
squeezed into the front
with all our luggage on one seat
as he had told us to.
A man asked who could speak English.
I was quiet.
It was dark.
He told us to be silent
or we would be shot.
We held our breath.
There wasn't a sound on that crowded bus.

As we approached, the plane made a huge noise,
like a C-130.
It opened at the back, a mouth.
We were thrown in like packets.
The pilot ordered *stop*
just as the last of our group was in.
Hundreds of us sat on the floor,
a huge string tied around us,
our babies on our laps.
Many were sick.

We arrived at Clark Field, Philippines, at 1:30 A.M.
Everyone was quiet.
We were handed medicine, blankets, mattresses.
People were everywhere.
There was much red tape,
name, sex, age.

I heard over the radio
soon after we left, the Vietnamese MPs,
not wanting any more people to leave the country,
arrested everyone at the airport.

THE
UNITED STATES:
GUAM
FORT CHAFFEE
NEW YORK CITY
GREENWICH
COS COB
1975-1980

GUAM

We flew the next day to Guam
packed in side by side
our possessions on our laps.
There, we slept on our luggage,
not knowing the other people,
afraid they would steal from us.
We were greeted by American officers,
who took us to a church,
and in bad Vietnamese
we could not understand
read us the regulations.
Most of the children were asleep.
We had been flying for hours and hours.
Still we had to line up for papers.
My granddaughter was sick with diarrhea.
She could not cry, not even suck.

In the acres and acres of tents,
blue-green nylon as far as the eye could see,
we had to find ours.
I was given a paper with our tent number.
We started walking in the bright sunlight,
carrying all the baggage and the sick baby.
Tiny stones on the path hurt my feet.
At the end of the long line of tents,
we could not find our number.
Since I was not afraid to speak English,
I was chosen to walk all the way back
over the stones
past the other tents
where people were settling in
under the burning sun.

CAMP

This time an American returned with me.
He could not find the number either.
Back I went to wait in the long lines.
I found our new number,
but the tent was not put up.
I laid the baby on a newspaper,
and we raised the tent ourselves.
As soon as it was up,
they called over the *haut-parleur*, the loudspeaker,
"Come fill out your papers."
We did not go. We did not care.
Too tired to move again, we fell asleep.

Much later, they called us for dinner
in English and in Vietnamese.
There was no time to wash.
Men and women shared the few bathrooms.
The women were so shy
they would go only at night.
In the day, we used a can
with water in it
just as at the market.

We waited in lines for food.
When it came,
we could not swallow some of it.
The rice was cooked in a way
that scared us,
very soft, filled with water and minced fish.
It had a horrible smell.
Even the children shook their heads.

The Americans spent a lot of money,
but they did not know our diet—
mostly fresh vegetables
and fruit with fluffy rice.
If you had money
there was "meals on wheels"
a cart from which they sold sandwiches,
hot dogs and ice cream.

LOST

We are a hot people from a hot country.
Even we could not take the Guam sun
burning through the nylon tent.
Our family collected empty food boxes
left by the Americans.
We put them on the roof to shield the sun.
Others near us copied the idea.

The magazine did not know where we were.
Half of my family did not know.
I had everyone make signs with colored pencils.
We all worked, putting them on tents,
nailing them to trees.

The sign said,
"Nga is in Tent 1005
at location such and such.
Please get in touch."
We heard nothing.

Once in a queue for food,
I saw my nephew, who called,
"Auntie, Auntie, I am out.
My wife and children are stuck behind.
I must fill the papers."
Then he was swallowed by the door.

Many families were separated.
Children wandered from tent to tent
crying for their parents.

SAIGON FALLS

On the night of the 30th
we heard on the little radio I always carried
that Big Minh, the last president of South Vietnam,
had given up.

Sitting on the floor of the blue tent in Guam,
all of us cried, even the boys.
We had thought we would be gone only a short time.
Now we knew we would never return,
never see our friends and family.
Our country was lost.

We worried about Bao, my sister, the other children.
All night long, whenever we'd see the lights of a bus
driving by with other refugees,
we'd go out to ask about our relatives.
I never saw a familiar face.

Americans forget
there are all kinds of Vietnamese,
fishermen, farmers
doctors and lawyers
educated and uneducated.
We lived in constant fear of being robbed
by our own countrymen.

FORT CHAFFEE

After days and days
I saw Harold from the office
driving down the long rows of tents
calling out my name.
We told him what we needed
and he returned with powdered milk,
20 pairs of rubber sandals,
(ours were ruined by the tiny stones)
oranges and apples.
When the children saw the fruit,
they jumped up and down saying,
"Now we will survive.
We have fruit!"

Harold promised to help us with the paperwork.
Before we left Saigon, our family made a plan
to meet in California.
I did not know California
but I thought it was a warm place.
We wrote *San Francisco* on our papers.

On the way to the airport,
I read on my papers *Fort Chaffee*.
I asked the officer, "What does this mean?"
He answered, "Fort Chaffee means Fort Chaffee.
You are going to Arkansas."
I said, "But I want to go to San Francisco."
"You have no choice," he said.
We resigned ourselves to going
though we did not know what it meant
or how it would be.
"Don't be worried," Linh said,
"We have our mouths. We can talk."

Many people were sick on the flight.
We arrived at 3 A.M.
went right to work on the papers.
There were eight people at the desk.
For hours they asked about our private lives.
We were treated like beasts
standing to sleep
standing in categories—
Files, Pictures, Health.

Finally we were settled,
eight of us—all in one room.
We were almost asleep
when the loudspeaker called out,
"Everybody up to do the paperwork."
They threatened to send us back to Vietnam.
I said, "Send us back. I do not care.
I will not move. I cannot move."

BAO

My daughter volunteered to translate
so she could see the lists of newcomers
hoping to find word of the family.

With 20,000 people, Fort Chaffee was overflowing.
For days and nights we did paperwork.
I helped others who did not speak English.

I worried about Bao and my sister
but could only say with the fates,
"If they're lucky, they'll make it."

One day the New York office called
and spelled Bao's name over the phone.
He had called the Red Cross.

They were in Indian Town Gap, Pennsylvania.
My sister had been separated from the group
and ended up on Wake Island.

I had mixed feelings,
happy she was out,
unhappy I could not live with Bao.

VIETNAMESE GENERAL

I recognized a general.
He was said to have been one of the richest
men in Vietnam.
If you did not want to be enlisted,
you would pay him money.
If you did not want to be transferred
to the battlefield,
you would pay him money.
If you wanted your husband, or brother, or son
to go abroad for further training,
you would pay him money.
He was said to have over 100 million dollars.

One morning in the camp
a mob of women came up to him.
They took off their high-heeled wooden shoes
and began beating him about the head
screaming, "Because of you, my son,
my brother, my husband was left behind."
They beat him
until the MPs came and stopped them.

LIFE AT FORT CHAFFEE

Our food was dished out
with an ice-cream scoop.
There were no vegetables
but we learned fast what was good.

Word would go around,
"Beef today, get the beef."
"Canned fish, no good."
The children took extra apples
on apple days.

We could buy ham sandwiches
candy bars and ice-cream on a stick
at a small snack bar
called "The Hitching Post."

By the second month we enjoyed ourselves.
The couple next to us had a stove
and access to outside food.

We cooked chicken, ready-made soup,
toasted soft white American bread
until it was hard like French bread.

My granddaughter recovered
drinking special milk from a can
with a smiling blond mother and baby
photographed on pink paper.

We saw Elizabeth Taylor
and Sophia Loren on a huge outdoor screen—
all of us sitting on the grass
watching movies in the sky.

My son fell in love
with Linh's daughter.
We saw them sneak off
into the night holding hands.

Linh spent his days fishing
in a small brook behind the barracks.
He used a branch, string
and a paper clip made into a hook.
Once he caught a snake.

FAREWELL TO
FORT CHAFFEE

We did not know why our papers took so long.
Maybe the authorities had to go to Washington
to see if we had ever been in jail in Vietnam.
They asked about our business, our schooling,
our private lives. I told everything.

When my bossman from the magazine arrived,
the red tape disappeared.
He arrived on a Saturday.
After months of waiting,
the papers came out of hiding.
We could leave the next day.

By now we loved our barracks
had made friends with other people.
A woman near us,
a bar-girl from the countryside,
wanted my address.
She said she was alone
and would need friends once out of the camp.
Her husband was an American GI
who said he would pick her up
in Naples, Florida.

We all sat on the porch
talked about our country
and wondered about our future.
Some of us would go East
and some West,
wherever there was work.

THE RAMADA INN

We drove in three cars
past the armed guards
out of the gates of Fort Chaffee
down the highway to the Ramada Inn.

With only two of us in a room,
a colored T.V., a private bathroom
and a swimming pool,
it seemed like a palace.

We sat at a long table
eating like we would never eat again.
Only the lovers were sad.
Linh and his family were going to California,
my family and I to New York.

NEW YORK CITY

We stayed at the Alden Hotel
on the West Side of New York City.
My son was fascinated.
"How big it is,"
he kept saying
looking out the windows
at the tall houses,
"like huge boxes of matches."

I would not let them down on the street.
I knew New York was full of crime
especially in the dark.
The children asked what floor we were on.
"Sixteen," I answered.
They said in awe,
"This is so much bigger than our Caravelle Hotel."

We heard a knock.
I hurriedly opened the door.
Our friends warned,
"Never open a door like that.
One day you will get into trouble.
In this country, first look
through the small hole
and then open the door."
They brought us chopsticks,
nuoc mam, and bags of oranges.

THE OFFICE

After a Chinese dinner, our American friends
showed me the office building
all made of glass
with fountains on the outside.
In the night my eyes looked
up and up into the sky
at the hundreds of lit windows.
The children said,
"Mummy, will you work here
in this huge building?"
I said yes,
but I was scared.
I was not good at figures.
I had to feed my children.
By the third day
I was at work
on the 27th floor
in Accounts Payable.

MY BROTHER'S ESCAPE

When we were reunited with my younger brother
he told us he and his family
could not leave by the airport.
The rocketing was too heavy.
They went by sampan from Nha Be.

After floating eight days and nights
with no food and little water,
they were picked up by an American battleship.
To board they had to climb a rope one by one
while the huge ship pitched from side to side
on the rough seas.

Everyone wanted to be first up the rope.
People crawled over other people.
Many fell into the ocean.
His wife was pregnant
does not know how she found strength
to climb the rope.

No one could carry anything.
Fathers threw their babies up to the mothers.
With luck they made it.

Two months after I left the base
my brother ended up in Fort Chaffee
in my same room!
The woman next door asked,
"Do you know Mrs. Nga? You look like her."
"She is my sister," he replied.

THE CHURCH

The church helped us find a place to live.
We were afraid the community would not understand us,
so many people living together—Asians.
In New York City, the places we wanted to live in
were too expensive, the cheap places too dangerous.
A kind family let us live in their house
in Connecticut, which is a good place
full of green grass and birds singing.
If we could be together, we were happy.

When the church ladies came to talk,
I was afraid to tell them about the two wives.
Bao and my sister and their children
had gone from the camps to Massachusetts
where they had contacts.
I talked to the church women about ordinary things,
not my whole life.

They warned me not to let my little grandchildren
watch "The Incredible Hulk" on the television.
They said they admired me, making "do" on my own.
They said we were a brave family,
honest and hardworking.

We needed the church.
Without it, the houses we read of in the papers
would shut their doors to us.
We were grateful to the church.
They paid some of the rent,
but we are proud and do not like
finding our clothes at the rummage sale.
People will give one shoe to a rummage sale.

ALLISON

Our sponsors helped us find our first house
on Old Church Road in Greenwich, Connecticut.
I kept my little bottles of perfume
on the bureau in my bedroom.
My children teased me, saying,
"You thought there was no perfume
in the United States."

Through the church,
a family offered to tutor us in English.
At first they all came,
the husband, and the wife and the daughter, Allison.
My son studied with Allison.
She soon moved into his room.
We offered her our food and hospitality.
She criticized me, turned my son against me.

I rode the commuter train to New York every morning
leaving at 6:30, returning in the evening.
One night Allison said,
"I accept you as an educated woman.
How could you let yourself
become a second wife?"
I was shocked.
She was not my mother, not my sister
only a guest in my house.

They began to stay in his room all day,
never sharing meals with us
never talking to us
drinking and smoking
listening to loud music at night.
She played a guitar, slept late.

I could hear her step out of bed
over my head, above me.

I had to send for Bao in Massachusetts.
He said, "This is not a bar,
not a hotel. This is our home."
He threatened to throw the tape recorder
they played all night out the window.
She pushed my son to fight back.
"How can you let him talk to you that way?"
"He is my father," my son answered.

Finally the rest of us had to move
to get away from her.

MRS. LARSEN'S APARTMENT

After we talked about my life,
Mrs. Larsen said, "Nga, your father
should have named you
Phuong for phoenix, not Nga for swan."

She went to the red bookcase
took down two glass boxes.
In them lay perfect musical instruments,
miniatures, glued on purple brocade.

My father's masterpieces!

I'd watched him by the window in Cholon
as he sat hour after hour
carving the tiny violin bows
dying the silks himself.

He made one set for each child.
Even in old age, his eyes were perfect,
his hands steady.

The office staff had presented the Larsens
with a set when they left Saigon,
one of eastern instruments, one of western.
My brother had given the office his,
thinking Father could make him another.

"I wish I could help you more with your son.
I really don't know what you should do,
but I want you to have this," Mrs. Larsen said
and handed me the case with the ti ba and the sao.

She kept the western case.

DEATH DAY

Each year we celebrated my father's death day.
We burnt imitation money
so he would have it to spend,
paper clothes
so he would have them to wear,
left his favorite meals on the altar.

We did this
to show we had not forgotten him.
We did this
to teach his grandchildren
and his great-grandchildren
to respect their elders.

JOBS

We took the jobs available.
My son-in-law, who had a law degree,
sold the Electrolux vacuum cleaner
demonstrated door to door.
American people are afraid of Asians.
They would not let him in.

My sons worked as mechanics,
sold gasoline at night for extra money
until they were robbed.
My daughter worked in a training program
for a cosmetics company.
Bao and my sister started a small grocery store
near the university, selling notebooks, cigarettes,
cookies, ice cream, newspapers for the students.

My brother is an electrician.
My daughter-in-law stayed home
to cook and watch the babies.
We all studied English at night.
One of our friends in Saigon
was Chief Justice of the Supreme Court.
He was trained in France
spoke four languages.
He wrote me:
"I am a watchman in Houston.
When they hired me,
they felt uneasy with my title,
called me a telephone operator.
When anyone knocks on the door
of the company, I open it.
They call me a telephone operator,

but to tell you the truth,
I am a watchman."

From what I have seen in the States,
education means less than in my country.
There, if you are well educated,
you are sure of a high position and respect.
We say with the Chinese,
*"Learn to handle a writing brush
and you will not handle a begging bowl."*
Here a skilled worker makes a lot of money.
America is an industrial society.

TET IN AMERICA

The whole week of Tet
I prepared our favorite dishes
three times a day every day.
After the incense burned,
I removed the food from the altar,
put it on the table.

How silly I felt each noontime
alone in my house
surrounded by little saucers of food,
no one to share them with
no neighbors around me celebrating.

I'd asked my children to take time off
the way I had.
They said, "What for?
So we can sit around the table
and stare at each other?"

I said I did this not for them
but for our ancestors.
Inside I was sad
feeling myself on a desert
knowing my customs will die with me.

LETTER TO MY MOTHER

Dear Mother,

I do not know if you are receiving my letters, but I will keep writing to you as you are always in my mind.

We have been here three years now. I have moved from Greenwich and have a wooden shingled house in Cos Cob. We have a garden in the back where we plant vegetables, flowers in the front the way we used to when we were together. I have a pink dogwood tree that blooms in spring. It looks like the Hoa dai tree, but has no leaves, only flowers.

We worked for months to clear away the poison ivy, a plant that turns your skin red and makes you itch.

We are near a beach, a school and a shopping center. Green lawns go down to the streets and there are many cars and garages. I am even learning to drive.

When we got our new house, people from the church came and took us to "Friendly's" for ice cream. Americans celebrate with ice cream. They have so many kinds—red like watermelon, green for pistachio, orange sherbet like Buddha's robes, mint chocolate chip. You buy it fast and take it away to eat.

Our house is small, but a place to be together and discuss our daily life. At every meal we stare at the dishes you used to fix for us and think about you. We are sorry for you and for ourselves.

If we work hard here, we have everything, but we fear you are hungry and cold and lonesome. Last week we made up a package of clothes. We all tried to figure out how thin you must be now. I do not know if you will ever receive that package wrapped with all our thoughts.

I remember the last days when you encouraged us to leave the country and refused to go yourself. You said you were too old, did not want to leave your home and would be a burden to us. We realize now that you sacrificed yourself for our well-being.

You have a new grandson born in the United States. Thanh looked beautiful at her wedding in a red velvet dress and white veil, a yellow turban in her dark hair. She carried the chrysanthemums you love.

You always loved the fall in Hanoi. You liked the cold. We don't. We have just had the worst winter in a century, snow piled everywhere. I must wear a heavy coat, boots, fur gloves, and a hat. I look like a ball running to the train station. I feel that if I fell down, I could never get up.

Your grandson is three, in nursery school. He speaks English so well that we are sad. We made a rule. We must speak Vietnamese at home so that the children will not forget their mother tongue.

We have made an altar to Father. We try to keep up our traditions so that we can look forward to the day we can return to our country, although we do not know when that will be.

Here we are materially well off, but spiritually deprived. We miss our country. Most of all we miss you. Should Buddha exist, we should keep praying to be reunited.

Dear Mother, keep up your mind. Pray to Buddha silently. We will have a future and I hope it will be soon.

We want to swim in our own pond.
Clear or stinky, still it is ours.

Your daughter,

Nga

LETTER FROM VIETNAM, HAND-CARRIED TO FRANCE, MAILED TO THE U.S.

Dear Daughters and Sons,

I received your letter and am glad you are happy. Here things are getting worse. We live from day to day. We have spent our savings, sold our antiques and jewelry. Last week your brother sold the last silver cup of the family.

We have to work very hard here now. There are so many new rules. Each family is allowed to change only 5000 piasters. Thousands of people became bankrupt, including us. Many killed themselves. Some put their money in sacks with stones and let it sink under the river rather than give it back to the government.

The government controls everything, food, clothes and housing. They put many people to live in your sister's house. Each family (not a comrade family) is allowed each month to buy at the official rate

> 1 dozen eggs
> 1 kilo of meat
> 10 kilos of rice
> 1 kilo of sugar

and 5 meters of material. The food lasts our family only a few days and then we must buy at the blackmarket rate which is 5 or 6 times higher.

Your brothers are not allowed to work for the government. They say jobs are scarce and are kept for the comrades. My retirement pension from your father is not paid. We are considered deserters, belonging to the old regime. We could not live without the money you send through our "friend."

We pray not to be sick. The hospital and all good medicine is not for us. It is for the comrades.

I must tell you, recently an order from the government said that all tombs in Saigon and its vicinity should be removed or they will be dug up. We will sacrifice anything, but not your father's tomb. Although it is on private land, I am worried.

I received the package three months after you sent it from the United States. The blouse is too big, but I wear it. The soup was all spoiled even in those little packages.

My favorite carnations are in full bloom. I think of when we were all together. I love my country, but I miss my family. Please let me come with you.

Your Mother

BLUE CABLE

Washington D.C. accepted my application.
My mother had a chance to come to America.
My heart sang.
Back from work, I shared the news with my family.

Everyone wanted her.
We agreed she would stay three months with each group.
We carried our happiness everywhere
even in our dreams.

Late April. I was in the backyard in the garden
admiring my new red tulips.
The postman had me sign a blue cable.

"Mother died. March 26. Funeral Saturday."

My mother dead for one month.
My mother so far away
did our relatives perform the ceremony?
Did they dig her tomb deep?

O my country!

O my countrymen
so many of you left in shallow graves
in time of war
your souls wandering ceaselessly.

THE DEAD
MUST NOT GO HUNGRY

In Cos Cob, we worshiped Mother every day.
We made an altar in the living room
put up her picture, burnt incense
left a bowl of rice and one hard-boiled egg.

The dead must not go hungry.
From the egg will come a chicken
from the chicken an egg.
The dead will have plenty.

I looked at her picture,
the last one ever taken,
and thought of her children
in Hanoi, in Saigon, in the U.S.

Did my elder brother in Hanoi know of her death?
How many letters I had sent.
From him, only one short note saying,
"I thought you would want to keep this."

Attached was my father's note in 1954
explaining how he was moving to the South
because he believed the communists
would break up the family.

"If Buddha is good," he wrote,
"Pray for him to unify us.
One day we will be together again
in one country."

I stared at my mother's picture

saw the translucent blue jade bracelet
she always wore on her left wrist.

We have a saying,
*"You do not know how beautiful your jade is
when you are wearing it."*

"Mother," I prayed, "Your one hundred days are past.
We invite your spirit
to go to the pagoda in Washington
where Buddha will take care of your soul."

WASHINGTON PAGODA

There were no dragons, no phoenix on the roof
no good and evil spirit-gods
guarding the front door.

Just a red two-storied house with pine trees in the front
a parking lot in the back.
A young woman in brown monk's robes greeted us.

In the central room a golden Buddha sat on a platform
his head reaching to the ceiling.
Burning sandalwood drifted through the room.

We changed into our white funeral clothes,
washed off our lipstick and makeup.
The monk entered and read Mother's names out loud,

her maiden name, her married name, her death date.
He recited all her good deeds
then summoned her soul to be with Buddha for a blessing.

At the sound of a bell,
we stood and chanted, kneeled and prayed.
I thought of Saigon.

Was my father's tomb still intact
with the white elephants at the four corners?
Did they bury my mother next to him
under the jackfruit trees
near the pagoda she loved?

The ceremony was over.
We packed our mourning clothes

into a little suitcase
and climbed into the second-hand stationwagon.

Looking out the window
at the lights on the New Jersey Turnpike
I prayed that we children

though across the world from one another
had followed the ancient traditions
so her spirit would rest with Father's in Paradise.

NEW YORK
CITY
1980

IN THE AMERICAN MUSEUM
OF NATURAL HISTORY

An equestrian statue of Theodore Roosevelt
guards the entrance.
On one side stands an Indian,
on the other a Negro.
Roosevelt rises head and shoulders above them,
his bronzed gunbearers.
The Negro exposes a naked leg,
the Indian a bare shoulder;
he wears moccasins, the Black, sandals.
Roosevelt wears boots and spurs and packs a pistol.
Behind the groomed tail of the horse,
swings a red dragon on an orange banner
announcing the opening of the Hall of Asian Peoples.

To reach the rooms
Mrs. Nga and I pass through
the darkened Hall of Asiatic Mammals.
Each diorama lights a world.
We stop before a leopard killing a peacock.
The bird's neck is broken
snapped against a rock.
The leopard stares straight ahead.
His mate watches from below.
Copper feathers lie upon the ground,
their turquoise eyes stare out.
A pair of peacocks flies into the painted jungle.

We find the Hall of Asian Peoples
just past the elephants.
Finding Vietnam is more difficult;
one small window

buried between India and China.
Black-and-white drawings show
a traditional wedding procession,
a typical farmer plowing with a water buffalo,
rice growing in a Vietnamese landscape,
four Vietnamese faces.
The only statue is a grinning Money God.
Its caption says
small change is dropped in his back for good luck.

Leaving the Hall of Asian Peoples,
Mrs. Nga smiles as she says,
"I think your country wants to forget about mine."

I picture us, Ba Larsen and Madame Nga,
arm in arm walking through the skeleton
of the dinosaur upstairs.
She has a flute and I a drum.
We carry no flags
and we make a sad song
as we pluck on the bones
dancing over the sides of the universe
past the bison and the bear
and the five-clawed dragon
and its burning pearls of wisdom.

NOTES

GLOSSARY

ANGKOR WAT: Magnificent temple complex in Cambodia, built in the twelfth century

AO DAI: Vietnamese silk dress, worn over long black or white pants

ARVN: (Pronounced R-VEN) Army of the Republic of Vietnam

BA: Mrs. or Lady

BETEL: A climbing pepper plant whose leaves wrapped around the nut from a betel palm and combined with the bark of a tree and lime is chewed as a stimulant

CA DAO: Vietnamese folk poem

CERCLE SPORTIF: Private Saigon club with swimming pool and tennis courts frequented by Vietnamese and foreigners

CHA GIO: Vietnamese egg roll

CYCLO: Tricycle cab

DMZ: Demilitarized zone dividing North and South Vietnam

DURIAN: A large oval fruit having a delicious flavor and an offensive odor

DUST OFF: Medical evacuation helicopter

GAMELAN: An East Asian percussion instrument, akin to the xylophone

GVN: Government of South Vietnam

HAMBURGER HILL: Peak of Apbia mountain in the Ashau Valley near the Laotian border, so named because the grinding battle there killed and wounded so many GI's

HOA SEN: Lotus

I CORPS: (Pronounced eye corps) the northernmost of the four military regions in South Vietnam

JACKFRUIT: A large East Indian tree bearing immense fruit. It is related to the breadfruit tree.

JUSPAO: Joint U.S. Public Affairs Office

KHE SANH: Once an outpost to recruit local tribesmen. Resupplied by General Westmoreland with Marine battalion. Scene of controversial and costly siege of the Marines by the North Vietnamese in 1968.

KHMER ROUGE: Communist guerrillas in Cambodian countryside, so named by Prince Sihanouk

KIM VAN KIEU: Nguyen Du's classic verse novel of filial devotion, written in 1813. Thuy Kieu, the heroine and eldest daughter, sacrifices herself, leaving behind her true love, Kim Trong, to marry her younger sister, Thuy Van, while she suffers slavery and prostitution to save her father. The title comes from the three different characters.

KIT CARSON SCOUTS: Vietnamese military defectors who worked with U.S.

LAM SON: Ancient Vietnamese triumph over China

LONGAN: A pulpy fruit related to the lichee

MACV: (Pronounced MAC-V) Military Assistance Command Vietnam. U.S. military headquarters in Vietnam, formed in 1962.

MAN IN THE MOON: In Vietnamese legend, the Man in the Moon ties couples together with the red thread of the marriage bonds.

MANGOSTEEN: Dark, reddish fruit. It has a thick rind and is very juicy.

MADAME NHU: Wife of Ngo Dinh Nhu, brother of Ngo Dinh Diem, President of South Vietnam

NLF: National Liberation Front

NUOC MAM: Favorite Vietnamese sauce made from fermented fish

NVA: North Vietnamese Army

PACIFICATION: A complex U.S. program of security and economic measures started in 1958 for government control of the villages. Elaborate systems such as the "Hamlet Evaluation System" were created to measure success at winning Vietnamese "hearts and minds."

PIASTERS: Vietnamese money. In 1970, 118 to the U.S. dollar; blackmarket 175.

PHO: Vietnamese soup

PLAIN OF JARS: High plain in the center of Laos where hundreds of urns 2,000 years old, thought to be funeral urns, were found. Scene of frequent battles and U.S. air raids.

PUNGI STICK: A bamboo stick about 20 inches long, used as a kind of booby trap by the Viet Cong. Both ends were sharpened. One end was buried about 6 inches deep; the other, having previously been dipped in human excrement, was exposed.

R&R: Rest and Recreation. Since Vietnam was considered a hardship post, every six weeks or so, depending on company policy, journalists got a week's vacation somewhere else in Asia.

RUFF-PUFFS: Vietnamese regional and popular forces. (RF's and PF's.) Regional forces were company size and protected district areas; popular forces were platoon size and protected home villages.

SAO: Flute

TET: Vietnamese New Year, at the end of January or the beginning of February, based on the lunar calendar.

TI BA: Oval-shaped mandolin

TITI: Pidgin for *petit*

USAID: United States Agency for International Development

WHITE MICE: Saigon police, so called because of their white gloves and shirts and apparent lack of martial spirit

WORLD: What the GIs called the U.S.

VIETNAM: A CHRONOLOGY

LEGEND OF ORIGINS

Once upon a time
Lac Long Quan, the King of the Dragons,
married Au Co, the Queen of the Fairies.
She gave birth to one hundred eggs
from which came one hundred children.

Then Lac Long said,
"I am a dragon. I like the sea.
You are a fairy. You like the mountains.
We cannot live together.
Let us divide the children and part."

He took fifty children to the Southern Sea
the other fifty went north with their mother
to the mountains near Hanoi.
There, the eldest male was elected king
beginning the Hong Bang dynasty
which lasted 2,000 years.

2897–258 BC	Hong Bang dynasty. Country was known as Van Lang.
257–208 BC	Thuc Dynasty. Country known as Au Lac.
208 BC	Trieu Da, a Chinese general, conquers Au Lac in Northern Vietnam. Proclaims himself emperor of "Nam Viet," Land of the Southern Viets, a people of Mongolian origin who had migrated south.
III BC–39 AD	1st Chinese Occupation. Nam Viet incorporated into Chinese empire as Giao Chi.
40–43	Trung sisters lead major insurrection against Chinese. Set up independent state, lasting only two years.
43–544	2nd Chinese Occupation. In 248, 23-year-old Trieu Au, the Vietnamese Joan of Arc, wearing gold armor and riding an elephant, leads another revolt against China.

603–939	3rd Chinese Occupation.
939–967	Ngo Quyen drives Chinese out. Becomes emperor, establishing Ngo Dynasty, beginning 900 years of Vietnamese independence.
968	After defeating the other 11 warlords, Dinh Bo Linh proclaims himself emperor. Calls his state Dai Co Viet, Kingdom of the Watchful Hawk, but pays tribute to China.
1010–1225	Ly Dynasty. Ly Thai To proclaims himself emperor. Moves to the new capital, Thang Long (now Hanoi). Thang Long means "a dragon rising up," from a dream the emperor had about the place.
1225–1400	Tran Dynasty. Tran Hung Dao defeats the Mongols twice.
1306	The king of the Champa, the Indianized kingdom of central Vietnam, gives up Thua Thien province to the Tran, beginning the southward march of the Vietnamese.
1414–1427	Chinese Occupation (Ming dynasty).
1428	Emperor Le Loi, Vietnam's great hero, defeats China.
1460–1497	Le Thanh Tong rules. Initiates many legal reforms.
1553–1788	Two and a half centuries of civil strife between regional factions. 1627 first of many clashes between the Trinh rulers in the North and the Nguyen in the South.
1787	Pigneau de Behaine, Bishop of Adran, leads an expedition to back his protégé, the Nguyen leader Nguyen Anh. Louis XVI at first finances the expedition and then withdraws his support.
1788	Nguyen Hue defeats the Chinese in Hanoi. Overthrows the last of the Le.
1802	Nguyen Anh becomes emperor under the name Gia Long. Calls country Vietnam. Bao Dai is a descendent of Gia Long.
1862	Treaty of Saigon. French acquire Cochin China (Mekong Delta area).
1883	Treaty of Hue. French protectorate extended to include Tonkin (North Vietnam) and Annam (Central Vietnam).
1887	Cochin China, Cambodia, Annam and Tonkin administratively united as Indochinese Union.
1900	French control all levels of administration.
1927	Viet Nam Quoc Dan Dang, Vietnamese Nationalist Party, organized in North. Founded by Nguyen Thai Hoc.
1930	Yen Bai uprising by the VNQDD. French reprisal fierce. VNQDD leaders guillotined.
	The Indochinese Communist Party under Nguyen Ai Quoc, better known as Ho Chi Minh, established in Hong Kong.
1932	Bao Dai, theoretically emperor since 1925, returns to Vietnam from France to ascend the throne under French.
1940	Japanese enter Vietnam after France falls to Germany. New Vichy government gives Japanese right to move through Indochina in return for Japanese recognition of French sovereignty there.
1941	Ho Chi Minh forms Viet Nam Doc Lap Dong Minh Hoi, called Viet Minh Front. Fights Japanese and French.
1945	**FEB.–MARCH** Two million people die of famine in the north. **MARCH** Japanese unseat French in Indochina and declare Cambodia, Laos and Vietnam independent under Bao Dai.

	JULY	Potsdam Agreement. Chinese Kuomintang occupy North Vietnam for six months to supervise the surrender of Japanese troops in North Vietnam. British to disarm them in the south.
	AUG.	Viet Minh occupies Hanoi.
	SEPT.	Ho Chi Minh proclaims Democratic Republic of Vietnam.
	OCT.	French return, reconquer much of South Vietnam. Viet Minh resist.
1946		Indochina War begins between French and Viet Minh.
1949	JULY	With French approval, Bao Dai forms the first government of the state of Vietnam.
	OCT.	Mao Tse Tung achieves victory in China.
1950		President Truman signs legislation granting $15 million in military aid to the French war in Indochina.
		35 American advisors are sent to Vietnam.
1954	MAY 7	French defeated by Ho's forces at Dien Bien Phu.
	JUNE	Diem named Prime Minister by Bao Dai.
	JULY	Geneva Agreement. French and Democratic Republic of Vietnam meet at international conference of Great Britain, United States, Soviet Union, and China plus State of Vietnam, Kingdom of Cambodia, Kingdom of Laos (called Three Associated States of Indochina). Agree to divide Vietnam at 17th parallel. Both sides to evacuate troops. Truce declared. People given 300 days to decide whether to live in the North or the South. Elections to be held in 1956 to reunify the country.
	SEPT.	The Southeast Asia Treaty Organization (SEATO) formed by the United States, Great Britain, France, Australia, New Zealand, Pakistan, Thailand, Philippines for defense of Southeast Asia.
1955	JAN.	U.S. sends direct aid to Saigon government and agrees to train South Vietnamese army.
	MARCH–SEPT.	Ngo Dinh Diem consolidates his power by putting down various sects, the Cao Dai, the Hoa Hao, and the Binh Xuyen. The Cao Dai was a fusion of Confucianism, Taoism and Buddhism modeled on the Catholic Church with a "pope" as head. They claimed 2 million followers, an army of 20,000 and controlled much of the Delta. The Hoa Hao, another political-religious sect of reformed Buddhists, had 1 million followers and an army of 15,000. The Binh Xuyen were gangsters, with an army of 25,000, who controlled the Saigon police and underworld.
	JULY	Diem rejects Geneva Accords and refuses to participate in nationwide elections.
	OCT.	National referendum held in the South. Bao Dai deposed. Diem promotes himself Chief of State.
1956		New constitution adopted by referendum in 1956. Diem elected 1st President of the Republic of Vietnam in accordance with the new constitution.

1957	OCT.	Communist insurgent activity in South Vietnam begins.
1960	APRIL	North Vietnam imposes universal military conscription.
	DEC.	National Liberation Front for South Vietnam officially born.
1961	NOV.	Kennedy increases military advisors to 16,000 over a two-year period.
1962	FEB.	American Military Assistance Command formed in South Vietnam.
1963	MAY	Buddhists demonstrate against Diem's discrimination.
	NOV. IST	Coup against Diem and Nhu.
	NOV. 2	Diem and Nhu assassinated.

U.S. aid increased to $500 million by that year.

1964	AUG. 2	Johnson Administration reports the USS *Maddox* attacked by North Vietnamese PT boats in Tonkin Bay.
	AUG. 7	Tonkin Gulf Resolution passed in Congress, giving Johnson extraordinary power to act in Southeast Asia.
1965	FEB.	President Johnson orders air attacks on North Vietnam. "Operation Rolling Thunder."
	MARCH	Marines land in Danang; first American combat troops.
	DEC.	American troops number approximately 184,000 in Vietnam.
1967	SEPT.	Nguyen Van Thieu elected President.
		U.S. spending more than $2 billion per month on the war.
1968	JAN.	Tet Offensive. Viet Cong and North Vietnamese attack U.S. Embassy in Saigon and 36 of the provincial capitals.
	MAY	U.S. and North Vietnam hold first formal negotiating session in Paris.

At the end of the year, American troop strength in Vietnam stands at 540,000.

1969	JAN.	NLF, North Vietnam, South Vietnam and U.S. agree to meet in Paris.
	JUNE	Nixon and Thieu meet on Midway. Nixon announces 25,000 troops will be withdrawn from South Vietnam by the end of August and emphasizes increased "Vietnamization," South Vietnam taking on additional responsibilities for the war.
	JULY	In Guam, Nixon proclaims "Nixon Doctrine" saying that in the future, unless a major power intervened in a Third World conflict, the U.S., to avoid situations such as Vietnam, will limit its assistance to economic and military aid rather than direct combat involvement.
1970	MARCH	Prince Norodom Sihanouk deposed as ruler of Cambodia. General Lon Nol heads new government.
	APRIL–JUNE	U.S. and South Vietnamese soldiers invade sanctuaries in Cambodia.
1971	FEB.	South Vietnamese invade Laos with U.S. support.
	JUNE–JULY	Secret peace negotiations with North Vietnamese begun by Kissinger.
	OCT.	Thieu reelected President.
1972	AUG.	Last U.S. ground combat troops leave Vietnam.
	DEC.	U.S. bombing of area around Hanoi and Haiphong.

1973	JAN.	Paris Accords signed between Kissinger and Le Duc Tho. The cease-fire begins on Jan. 28.
	MARCH	Last U.S. military personnel leave Vietnam.
	APRIL	American prisoners of war released in Hanoi.
1974	JAN.	Thieu declares war has begun again.
1975	APRIL 17	Phnom Penh falls to the Khmer Rouge.
	APRIL 21	Thieu resigns. Flees Saigon to Taiwan. Now lives in Great Britain.
	APRIL 30	Fall of Saigon.
1976		Vietnam is officially unified as Socialist Republic of Vietnam.

VIETNAMESE NAMES

Because there are less than a hundred family names in Vietnam, the Vietnamese use their given name as we do our family name. Take, for instance, Tran Thi Nga: *Tran* is the family name, *Thi* means female, and *Nga* is the given name. Married women use their husband's given name. Working married women use their own given names, but in society are called by their husband's name.

SOURCES

The two poems, "Lament of the Warrior's Wife" by Dang Tran Con on page 123 and the ca dao "Poor Matchmaking" on page 166 are from *A Thousand Years of Vietnamese Poetry*, edited by Nguyen Ngoc Bich, translated by Nguyen Ngoc Bich with Burton Raffel and W. S. Merwin, Alfred A. Knopf, New York, 1975.

The military expressions are from the *Cam Nang Thong-Dich Vien Quan-Doi, English-Vietnamese Military Handbook*, Vu-Anh-Tuan.

The description of Vietnamese as a tonal language is from The Vietnamese Culture Series, No. 2, Nguyen Dinh Hoa, Vietnamese Language Series, Department of Education, Republic of Vietnam, 1961.

The chronology is based on the following works:

Committee of Concerned Asian Scholars. *The Indochina Story*. Bantam, 1970.

Cooper, Chester L. *The Lost Crusade*. Dodd, Mead & Co., 1970.

Doan Them. *The Past Twenty Years*. Nam Chi Tung Thu, 1966.

FitzGerald, Frances. *Fire in the Lake*. Little, Brown, 1972.

Herring, George C. *America's Longest War: The United States and Vietnam, 1950–1975*. Alfred A. Knopf, 1979.

Karnow, Stanley. *Vietnam. A History*. Penguin Books, 1984.

Tran Trong Kim. *Summary History of Vietnam*. Tan-Viet-Saigon, 1958.